W9-BZY-868

GEORGE HERBERT MEAD

A Unifying Theory for Sociology

John D. Baldwin

Masters of Social Theory
Volume 6

Cover Photo: Historical Picture Service

SAGE PUBLICATIONS
The Publishers of Professional Social Science
Newbury Park   Beverly Hills   London   New Delhi

For Richard Golden
1947-1985
a person who cared about the important things
and led his life accordingly

For information address:

SAGE Publications, Inc.
275 South Beverly Drive
Beverly Hills, California 90212

SAGE Publications Inc.
2111 West Hillcrest Drive
Newbury Park
California 91320

SAGE Publications Ltd.
28 Banner Street
London EC1Y 8QE
England

SAGE PUBLICATIONS India Pvt. Ltd.
M-32 Market
Greater Kailash I
New Delhi 110 048 India

Printed in the United States of America

Library of Congress Cataloging-in-Publication Data

Baldwin, John D., 1941-
  George Herbert Mead: a unifying theory for
sociology.
  (Masters of social theory; v. 6)
  Bibliography: p.
  1. Mead, George Herbert, 1863-1931.   2. Sociology—
United States.   I. Title.   II. Series.
HM22.U6M373   1986   301'.092'4   85-30249
ISBN 0-8039-2821-X
ISBN 0-8039-2820-1 (pbk.)

FIRST PRINTING

Contents

X30263

Series Editor's Introduction

In this sixth volume of the Sage Masters of Social Theory series, John Baldwin offers an original analysis of George Herbert Mead's thought. For too long, I think, Mead's important ideas have been interpreted as primarily "social psychological." True, Mead's famous course on social psychology at the University of Chicago became enshrined with the posthumous publication of *Mind, Self, and Society*, and to this day, the ideas in this classic work constitute the basic core of our knowledge about the process of interaction. To have unlocked the mysteries of such a fundamental process is, of course, a substantial intellectual accomplishment, as Baldwin explores in Chapters 6, 7, and 8. Yet, Mead accomplished much more. For Mead was a philosopher who had a grand vision that typically is ignored in analyses of his thought. Indeed, Baldwin rightly reminds us that we cannot appreciate fully the power of Mead's analyses of "mind, self, and society" without placing his ideas on interaction into a larger intellectual context.

Baldwin has summarized this broader vision in Mead's work; and he has gone so far as to view it as a potentially unifying theory that brings together in one conceptualization the biology of the individual, the ecology of the physical environment, the processes of covert and overt behavior, the production and reproduction of micro structures, and, finally, the creation and maintenance of the macro-institutional structures of society. This re-introduction and analysis of Mead's grand unifying theory marks, I believe, an important contribution not only to our view of G. H. Mead, but also to sociological theory in general.

In reintroducing Mead's larger philosophical project, Baldwin has also given us guidelines for resolving some of the stagnating controversies that currently haunt social theory. For example, Baldwin documents how Mead's ideas can be evolutionary without being vulnerable to now trendy attacks on evolutionism, how Mead's concepts can emphasize function without being open to now ritualized criticism of functionalism, and how Mead's faith in the capacity of science to resolve human social problems can persist without being clouded by the dreary rabble of today's "critical theorists."

In sum, the pages that follow represent a truly important contribution to our retrospective interpretation of Mead and to our present theoretical concerns about linking biology, ecology, behavior, interaction, and social organization. There is much to be learned from a more comprehensive reading of Mead's philosophical project. John Baldwin is t be commended for helping to make this reading and a potential reawakening possible.

—*Jonathan H. Turner*

Preface

"Theory is the most practical thing in the world."
—Oliver Wendell Holmes, Jr.

George Herbert Mead (1863-1931) was a philosopher, social scientist, and humanistic individual. He was a person of great vision, with the skill for synthesizing an enormous breadth of knowledge in an elegant, unified system. He developed a philosophy of science and a beautifully integrated social theory that are as important today as they were in his own time.

Mead's unified theory can be extremely useful to modern social science. Mead's theory successfully synthesizes micro and macro social processes, mental and physical events, academic and practical concerns. It has the potential to advance sociology from its present fragmented state to a unified, scientific discipline, bringing together such diverse schools of thought as symbolic interaction, cognitive theories, structuralism, historical sociology, economics, conflict theory, social change, systems theory, and ecological and biosocial sociology.

The primary goal of this book is to summarize Mead's work in a logical and systematic manner that shows the power—and continued relevance—of his ideas. I have attempted to make the book useful for undergraduates in hopes that the social scientists of the future can benefit from seeing the subtlety, elegance, and power of Mead's model of the individual and society. Given limitations of space, I have focused primarily on presenting the core ideas of Mead's philosophy and unified social theory as clearly as possible, rather than developing an extensive critique of the weak points of Mead's work or attempting to update it.

I am grateful to the University of Chicago Press for granting permission to quote extensively from Mead's works. In order to faithfully represent Mead's views, I have presented many of his key points in his own words. (Almost all the quotations in the book are from Mead.) In order not to distort the meaning of these quotes, every attempt has been made to present them in the same context as they were in the original. Readers who have learned about Mead's theories from the secondary literature may be surprised by some of the contents of this book. I hope these readers will seriously consider the numerous quotations and references to Mead's original work and turn to Mead's own writings to discover the full extent of his theories. In order to organize the wealth of diversity found in Mead's work, I have patterned my methods of organization and development in this book after Mead's own, which are presented in Chapter 4.

I wish to thank the following people who read a draft of the manuscript and gave valuable feedback. Dr. Tamotsu Shibutani provided sensitive comments about various subtleties of Mead's theoretical system and Mead's intellectual relationships with his colleagues in the Chicago School. Dr. Otis Dudley Duncan was generous in his comments on the internal consistency of Mead's ideas and helped me hone finer discriminations about numerous aspects of Mead's theory. Dr. Janice Baldwin shared in the hours of critical reading needed to polish the final manuscript. I regret that space constraints made the inclusion of an index impossible, but an index is available from the author.

1

Introduction

George Herbert Mead was one of the most creative and important contributors to the development of the distinctively American philosophy of pragmatism. John Dewey, Alfred North Whitehead, and other respected philosophers have agreed that Mead was "a seminal mind of the very first order" (Dewey, 1932: x1; Whitehead, 1938). Although a member of the Chicago school of pragmatism, Mead was an independent thinker who made numerous distinctive contributions to the development of philosophy and social science.

Although Mead was a philosopher, his work is of special value to social scientists. In sociology Mead is best known for his social theories of mind, self, and symbolic interactionism, demonstrating how subjective experience emerges through the use of significant symbols (Sahakian, 1974: 92f; Blumer, 1981; Martindale, 1981). However, as a pragmatist philosopher, Mead made a much larger contribution than is widely recognized: He developed a unified theory of society that integrates both micro and macro social events as they evolve and change over time. It is this unified theory that is the focus of this book. (Naturally, Mead's unified theory includes his work on mind, self, and social psychology as an integral part of the larger theoretical framework.)

Figure 1 presents an overview of Mead's theories,[1] showing how Mead integrated information on the biological individual, behavior (both covert and overt), micro and macro society, and broader environmental systems. The superscripts in the figure identify the order in which Mead organized the components of his theory. A biological individual (a) is born into social and physical environments (b, c, and d) and acquires from those environments (e, f, and g) a complex repertoire of covert and overt behavior (h) that influences and shapes (i, j, and k) both micro and macro society (b and c) and the broader environmental systems (d). Because there are multiple, interconnected, and nonstatic elements in the model, all the components of the system can interact and undergo dynamic changes over time. Thus, the model provides the basis for the development of a multifactor theory of social change and evolution.[2]

MEAD'S LIFE

A brief review of Mead's life provides useful background information for understanding his intellectual work.[3] George Herbert Mead was born on February 27, 1863, in South Hadley, Massachusetts, of puritanical New England stock. He died on April 26, 1931, at the age of 68. George's father, Hiram Mead, was a minister in the Congregational church, and in his later years he taught in the Theological Seminary at Oberlin, Ohio. George's mother, Elizabeth Storrs Billings, was a well-educated woman who taught at Oberlin College for two years and was president of Mount Holyoke College for ten years. George had an older sister, Alice, who married a minister.

Although little is known about George Herbert Mead's childhood, he was apparently "a cautious, mild-mannered, kind-hearted, rather quiet boy" (Miller, 1973: xii). During his undergraduate years at Oberlin College, Mead developed a close friendship with Henry Castle, who came from a wealthy, well-educated family that had extensive land holdings and political influence in Hawaii. During their college years, Castle and Mead discussed philosophical and religious topics at great length, becoming increasingly critical of religious beliefs that hinged on conceptions of the supernatural. They also explored a broad range of literature, poetry, and history. After graduating from Oberlin at the age of 20, Mead spent a brief period teaching grade school; but he was relieved of his job because he was dismissing too many of his rowdy students—on the assumption that they were not serious about learning. Next, Mead spent three years working with a surveying crew that laid out a 1100-mile-long railway line from Minnesota to Saskatchewan. During these years Mead gained considerable experience with civil engineering and acquired an appreciation of the power and practical utility of the scientific method (Miller, 1973: xiii).

At the age of 24, Mead joined his friend Henry Castle at Harvard and spent a year studying philosophy and psychology, along with Latin, Greek, and other subjects. At that time, Mead's philosophical interests lay in the romantic philosophers and Hegelian idealism, as taught by Josiah Royce. The next year, in 1888, Mead joined Henry

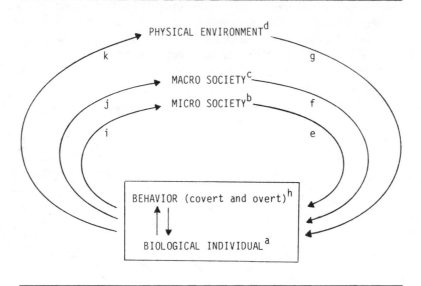

Figure 1: An Overview of the Components of Mead's Theoretical System

Castle and his sister, Helen, in Leipzig, Germany, where Mead focused his studies more on psychology than philosophy. He became especially interested in the work of Wilhelm Wundt and other physiological psychologists: The scientific study of the nervous system held possible keys for understanding the mind and resolving important philosophical problems. Wilhelm Wundt's theories of the gesture also provided Mead with a basic approach to communication that set the stage for his own later work on language, symbolic interaction, and human consciousness. After one year in Leipzig, Mead went to Berlin where he studied physiological psychology for two additional years; and all through his life he continued to interweave physiological concepts and data into various facets of his theories (see Chapter 5). In addition, the three years that Mead devoted to studying physiological psychology in Germany doubtless deepened his understanding and respect for science and helped him learn to think like a scientist.

During the period when Mead was studying in Germany, psychology was undergoing several major changes that had considerable impact on all his subsequent approaches to the study of psychology and philosophy. Darwin's evolutionary theory was not only causing a restructuring of biology, it was also stimulating more scientific and comparative approaches in psychology. The evolutionary perspective highlighted the relevance of scientific studies of animal behavior, especially with regard to the evolution of the nervous system and animal intelligence. Simultaneously, there were increasing criticisms of earlier introspective approaches to psychology, inasmuch as scientific and objective methods were proving to be considerably more useful in advancing the discipline. Mead was deeply influenced by these evolutionary and scientific trends in psychology. He often cited evolutionary theory and examples of animal behavior throughout his later work (Mead, 1899; 1908; 1910a; 1923; 1924-25; 1927b; 1929-30; 1934: 214f, 250ff; 1936: 127ff, 145-168, 270ff, 288ff, 301ff, 364-384, 411; 1938: 496f, 503f, 508f, 512, 515f), and he advocated objective methods for studying human behavior, consciousness, self-consciousness, and reflective intelligence (see Chapters 2-4). While Mead was in Germany, his continued philosophical discussions with Henry Castle and the scientific study of physiological psychology led Mead through a "quiet rebellion against the theological restraints of America" (Miller, 1973: xvii). In the process, Mead moved toward a purely scientific, naturalistic worldview devoid of nonempirical and supernatural concepts.

In 1891, after three years in Germany, Mead and Henry Castle's sister, Helen, were married. The two had first met at Oberlin ten years earlier, but they did not become seriously involved until the three years in Germany. At the time of his marriage, the 28-year-old Mead broke short his graduate training in Berlin (where he had been working toward a doctoral degree) to accept a position as instructor of philosophy and psychology at the University of Michigan. (He never completed his Ph.D.) He and Helen moved to Ann Arbor, Michigan, and one year later they had a son, whom they named Henry Castle Albert Mead.[4]

At Michigan, George Herbert Mead met John Dewey, and the two formed a close, strong, and long-lasting friendship. The two men shared many common interests and had long conversations in which they mutually stimulated each other's intellectual development and shared each other's psychological and philosophical theories. Mead and Dewey were in virtually complete agreement on all facets of their work, though each specialized in different areas and made his own unique contributions (Morris, 1970). Charles Cooley was also at Michigan, and Mead clearly adopted and expanded on some of Cooley's ideas—such as the "looking glass self"—though he rejected other facets of Cooley's work (Mead, 1914: 82; 1930b). James Hayden Tufts and other scholars at Michigan had their influence on Mead's intellectual development, too.

In 1892, Tufts moved to the newly founded University of Chicago (Morris, 1970). He suggested that John Dewey should be brought to

Chicago as head of the philosophy department. When Dewey came in 1894, he appointed Mead (who was 31 years old) as an assistant professor of philosophy. Angel, Moore, and Ames also joined the department, completing the core group of what was to soon be called "the Chicago school of pragmatism." Basically, pragmatism involves the application of the scientific method to psychological, sociological, and philosophical issues. Because of its much greater emphasis on social and ethical issues, the Chicago school of pragmatism was notably different from the other versions of pragmatism developed by Charles Peirce and William James: Peirce had a more logical-analytical orientation, and James a strongly individualistic approach (Morris, 1970: 178).

At Michigan and during the early years at Chicago, Mead expanded on Wundt's theories of the gesture by emphasizing the importance of social factors in the evolution and development of communication, role taking, mind, and self. This in turn led to the solution of several important epistemological and metaphysical problems (see Chapters 2 and 3). The success of both Mead and Dewey in applying evolutionary theory and scientific methods to psychological and philosophical issues hastened their expansion of pragmatism to deal with *all* ideas—even ethical and metaphysical ideas—as hypotheses that are open to empirical investigation (Mead, 1900/1964: 6f; 1929-30/1964: 385). Mead and Dewey focused on a broad range of philosophical, psychological, and sociological questions. In addition, they attempted to dovetail their theories with contemporary empirical work on evolution, animal behavior, physiology, physics, and other scientific topics. They were also widely read in the humanities—history, religion, the history of ideas, literature, poetry, art, aesthetics, ethics—and they applied their pragmatic philosophy to these topics, too. Although Mead focused primarily on philosophical, psychological, and sociological topics, he loved poetry, music, and the arts, and was quite knowledgeable in each area.

In 1905, Dewey left the University of Chicago and went to Columbia University. Mead continued to develop his theories of symbolic communication and human consciousness. Reflecting his broad range of interests, Mead taught a large number of courses on at least 13 different subjects, such as social psychology, nineteenth-century thought, Leibniz, German romanticism, Hegel, relativity, problems of philosophy, and ethics. Between 1910 and 1920, Mead worked on integrating Einstein's theory of relativity with his own thinking, attempting to bring unity to the entire scientific and pragmatic worldview. Gradually he pieced together an evolutionary cosmology that integrated all the sciences and resolved philosophical problems in terms of emergence—beginning with the emergence of the solar system and planets, then dealing with the evolution of life and increasingly higher levels of animal awareness, and culminating in human mind, self, and society. In the last fifteen years of his life, Mead turned increasing attention to macro societal issues and international relations, showing the interrelations of macro and micro social phenomena from a unified theoretical perspsective.

By the 1920's, his work had progressed to the point where it was clear that "Mead was the cosmologist of the late Chicago group" (Morris, 1970: 189). Near the end of his life, Mead was constructing an empirically grounded theory that integrated the central theories of physics, biology, psychology, and sociology, dealt with ethics, aesthetics and the philosophy of science, and resolved the problems of metaphysics and epistemology. Although Mead did not synthesize his ideas in a single systematic publication, a review of his written work and lectures (as presented in this book) supports Charles Morris's (1970: 188) conclusion that Mead was constructing such a system. The remainder of this book brings together the multiple strands of Mead's work in a systematic manner that follows his own methods of logical development. I have attempted to present the breadth of Mead's work in a model that captures the elegance and power of his pragmatic worldview.

Not only is pragmatism a powerful intellectual tool, it is easily applied to practical problems. Reflecting the social orientation of their academic work, the Chicago school pragmatists were socially active, concerned with producing reforms in education, social welfare, labor-management relations, treatment of immigrants, and so forth (Morris, 1970: 189f). In one of his early essays, Mead (1899) advocated the use of the scientific method as the best approach to social reform. Instead of guiding social change by a "vision given in the mount" or "a fixed idea of the world of the future," the scientific approach works by empirically evaluating various programs, selecting the most useful ones, and continually readjusting to the changing problems of an evolving social system (Mead, 1899; see also Mead, 1936: 240f, 363f). Mead was active in civic affairs and concerned with social problems, such as improving the schools, promoting vocational training, resolving labor problems, establishing Hull House and the Settlement House movement, supporting women's suffrage, and so forth (Mead, 1908a/1964: 88-90; 1908b; 1908-09; 1925-26; 1938: 454-457; Miller, 1973: xxi-xxxvii). In addition, he and his wife were exceptionally generous in helping students, friends, and relatives. In describing the Chicago school pragmatists, Morris (1970: 190) writes that they were committed men of high moral integrity. Their philosophic orientation and their social participation were of one piece. The philosophy they built and taught was the philosophy by which they lived.[5]

George Herbert Mead was a tall man of some 200 pounds. He believed in physical exercise and often jogged up and down the Midway. The people who knew him described him as kind, cheerful, mild mannered, soft spoken, and with no affectation or pretense (Ames, 1931; Miller, 1973). He was respected and held in high esteem by his colleagues and students. During the years that Mead taught at the University of Chicago, many sociologists sent their students to take his course on social psychology. As a result, an entire generation of Chicago sociologists was well informed about Mead's theories of mind, self, and social psychology; and many used and elaborated upon this subset of Mead's work. Unfortunately, the larger whole of Mead's pragmatic worldview and theories of macro society have not received full attention in sociology.[5]

When Mead died at age 68, he had published over 30 journal articles—along with several book reviews, abstracts, and so forth—but not a single book. After his death, many of the unfinished manuscripts, papers, and fragments that Mead had left in various degrees of completion were collected and published as books or "unpublished papers." In addition, copies of notes taken from his lectures on social psychology in 1914, 1927, and 1930 have been edited and published in book form (Mead, 1934; Miller, 1982). The 1934 book, *Mind, Self and Society* (based primarily on stenographic transcripts of his 1927 lectures on social psychology), has been the most widely read and cited of Mead's work, which again reinforces the idea that Mead's contribution was limited to social psychology.

* * *

George Herbert Mead was a pragmatist philosopher who developed a unified theoretical system that can integrate an enormous range of information on mind, body, language, intelligence, self, socialization, society, and social change. Mead's work could be of greater value to contemporary sociology than is often recognized. The present book will make the integrated whole of Mead's work more easily accessible.

Part I

Philosophical Foundations

Mead is often described as the founder of modern symbolic interactionism (Blumer, 1969; Manis and Meltzer, 1978; Heiss, 1981). In the sociological literature, he is usually described as a social psychologist who explained the emergence of mind and self through symbolic social interaction. Although these statements are true, they do not reflect the whole of Mead's intellectual contribution. Mead developed a philosophical system that allowed him to construct a social theory that unifies all facets of society and social experience—subjective and objective events, small-scale (micro) and large-scale (macro) social processes. This larger contribution may be just as valuable to the social sciences as is the social psychology for which he is better known.

Part I presents the philosophical foundations of Mead's unified theory, showing why he argued for a purely empirical approach to mind, body, self, society, and social change. It demonstrates how he succeeded in avoiding all the dualisms—especially mind-body dualism and the schism between the micro and macro level of social analysis—that have fragmented most social theories and prevented the development of unified social theories.

Part II presents the actual unified empirical model that Mead developed, based on the philosophical foundations described in Part I. Finally, Part III briefly describes several ways in which contemporary sociologists can utilize Mead's work to advance modern social science.

2

Pragmatism

To understand the context and direction of Mead's total life work, it is useful to examine the philosophical paradigm that he helped create and within which he worked. Pragmatism is in essence the extension of the scientific method to all areas of intellectual inquiry, including psychology, sociology, and philosophy. All ideas and theories are treated as hypotheses that can be tested for their ability to solve problems and provide useful information (Mead, 1929-30/1964: 385). Any idea—even ethical and aesthetic ones—can be evaluated in terms of the type of consequences that result from it (Mead, 1900; 1908; 1913; 1923; 1925-26; 1938: 454ff).

To avoid a common misunderstanding, let us make a clear discrimination between vulgar pragmatism and philosophical pragmatism. In everyday language, people often use the word "pragmatic" in reference to any practical, hard-nosed, matter-of-fact viewpoint or decision. Choices are based on practicality or expediency. A person who wants to get rich fast might use a vulgar pragmatic approach, making any kind of deals—legal or not—that promise to be lucrative. In contrast, the philosophical pragmatism created by Mead and the Chicago-school philosophers is an integrated philosophical system that is designed to advance all facets of human knowledge and improve the human condition by the rigorous application of scientific methods. As part of their system, Mead and Dewey developed humanistic ethical standards that are clearly oriented to resolving social and personal problems in a socially responsible manner that does not sacrifice the interests of one sector of society in favor of those of another sector (Mead, 1899; 1908; 1913; 1923; Dewey, 1891; 1922).

A SCIENTIFIC PHILOSOPHY

At the turn of the century, Mead and Dewey thought that pragmatism was the next logical step in the development of philosophy, though they faced considerable resistance from all sides (Moore, 1961: 1). In tracing the intellectual developments of the past three centuries, Dewey (1920: 75-76) noted that "roughly speaking" seventeenth-century science dealt with astronomy and general cosmology; eighteenth-century science with physics and chemistry; and nineteenth-century science with geology and biology. Only the moral and social issues remained to be analyzed scientifically. "Does it not seem to be the intellectual task of the twentieth century to take this last step? When this step is taken the circle of scientific development will be rounded out and the reconstruction of philosophy be made an accomplished fact." Early prescientific philosophies would be reconstructed in light of empirical data and placed on a firm scientific foundation. Science had proven to be more successful than any other method for gaining reliable and useful knowledge about the physical and biological world. The pragmatists set out to demonstrate the advantages of applying the scientific method to philosophy, psychology, and sociology.

Mead's (1929-30; 1936; 1938: 494-519) analysis of the history of philosophy led him to conclusions similar to Dewey's. Starting with the ancient Greeks, Mead stated that "ancient philosophy was entirely metaphysical." "Its dominant attitude was contemplation" (Mead, 1938: 513). The Greeks attempted to understand the ideal forms in a Platonic heaven—in the "supersensible world" (Mead, 1938; 504)—via logic, rational dialogue, and contemplation. Later, Renaissance thinkers mixed contemplation and scientific research in an attempt to decipher the "goal of the universe" (Mead, 1938: 513). This incongruous mixture of contemplation and science produced three problems: the problems of epistemology, mind-body dualism, and an apparent conflict of mechanism and teleology (Mead, 1938: 513f). One by one, the sciences abandoned contemplation (along with the philosophical puzzles created by mixing contemplation with empiricism), and developed a purely empirical orientation. In philosophy, only pragmatism solved the three problems of Renaissance philosophy by following the example of science and abandoning the use of contemplation. Mead concluded: "In my judgment only pragmatism has successfully completed the revolution. . . . " "But I speak as a pragmatist" (Mead, 1938: 514).

The emergence of science in the Renaissance reflected an increasing reliance on careful observation and analysis of *this* world. The prescientific, contemplative world tended to be "otherworldly" (Mead, 1936: 362; 1938: 504f, 515); and during the early Christian era, otherworldly knowledge was based on the dogma of the church. The emergence of science involved a turning away "from the dogma of the church" (Mead, 1936: 8) and "brought men back to observation" (Mead, 1936: 281). Scientific knowledge is based on data gleaned from observations of this world, where "the ground of authority lies in the knowledge which you yourself can in some sense grasp" (Mead, 1936: 11). Thus, science is based on data rather than dogma (Mead, 1936: 247, 259, 266, 360f; 1938: 92-100); "and, so far, science has always been successful in its conflicts with dogma" (Mead, 1936: 259).

Although Mead and Dewey believed that the twentieth century would see the extension of the scientific method into social and philosophic issues, this belief was not based on simple notions of historical determinism or a facile projection of past trends into the future. In his comparison of different forms of philosophy and means of gaining knowledge, Mead presented considerable evidence that the scientific method is superior to all other methods of gaining knowledge and regulating human affairs (Mead, 1917a; 1923; 1924-25; 1929a; 1932; 1936).[6] Science is superior to trial-and-error learning, introspection, a priori logic, religious dogma, idealism, speculative philosophy, and all other nonempirical sources of knowledge. Given that the scientific method is based on the continuous investigation of and readjustment to an ever-changing and evolving environment, it provides much more sensitive observations and up-to-date information than do philosophical rationalizations of prior beliefs, a priori logic, or dogma based on ancient thought (Mead, 1929a).

Mead's analysis of the evolution of consciousness and intelligence provided strong support for the hypothesis that the scientific method was superior to all other means of attaining knowledge. Taking an evolutionary perspective, Mead (1932: 68f) described consciousness as existing on a continuum from low levels of feeling in simple organisms to high levels of symbolic thought in humans, and he described the preconditions for the emergence of the successively higher levels of awareness and consciousness. When socially living humans began to use arbitrary symbols for communication and originated early languages, they created a tool that made possible the emergence of one of the most advanced levels of consciousness and intelligence, which Mead described as "reflective intelligence" (Mead, 1934: 90-109). When people learn language and talk with one another, each individual gains the ability to talk with himself or herself: "We can talk to ourselves, and this we do in the inner forum of what we call thought." "Our thinking is an inner conversation..." (Mead, 1924-1925/1964: 288). It is this inner conversation that makes reflective intelligence possible: Before acting, an individual can reflect on all the possible alternatives that are available, and select the alternative that appears—based on prior experience—to promise the best future outcomes (Mead, 1934: 100).

Reflective intelligence is much more efficient than the trial-and-error behavior seen in lower species. When a dog is trapped behind a fence, it may run around frenetically, in a trial-and-error search for some means of escape. When humans are caught in difficult situations, they often stop and reflect on several possible alternative solutions to their problem and evaluate each alternative in light of the available data. Reflective intelligence is much more economical than trial-and-error methods, as it avoids the time-consuming process of actually attempting to carry out each alternative before evaluating it, the way a dog does (Mead, 1927a: 154-155). For solving problems, reflective intelligence is also superior to speculative philosophy, a priori logic, and other idealistic modes of thought, because these latter strategies focus more on rationalizing one's beliefs than on solving problems that arise in the world of experience (Mead, 1929a).

For Mead, the fullest development of reflective intelligence is to be found in the scientific method: "Science is an expression of the highest type of intelligence, a method of continually adjusting itself to that which is new" (Mead, 1936: 290).[7] Scientists have developed reflective intelligence to a systematic method that is well-suited for exploring new topics, assimilating new data, and thereby constantly developing greater knowledge and power. As experiments continue to produce new data, previously accepted theories can be evaluated, criticized, reformulated, and retested. "The scientific method is that by means of which the individual can state his criticism, can bring forward the solution, and bring to it the test of the community" (Mead, 1936: 415). As numerous scientists suggest different hypotheses, reflecting their different perspectives on scientific problems (Mead, 1936: 405-417), the various hypotheses can be evaluated in light of the available data. "Science is tested by the success of its postulates. It brings its hypotheses to the test of experience itself; and if this test is met, then the doctrine is one to be accepted until some flaw can be found in it, until some new problem arises within it" (Mead, 1936: 258). "When the hypothesis works it ceases to be a hypothesis; it is reality,[8] not eternal, indefeasible reality, but the only reality with which we are acquainted..." (Mead, 1929a/1964: 331). Even after a hypothesis has been tested on multiple occasions and accepted as a theory, there is no guarantee that exceptions and anomalies will not arise in the future: "[I]t is still subject to some other chance exception. That is, it still remains hypothetical" (Mead, 1936: 285). "No statement that science makes is final" (Mead, 1936: 286). Over time, the body of currently accepted hypotheses grows and changes, usually becoming more refined, more powerful, and capable of producing greater adaptation to the environment (Mead, 1936: 371f).

Not only is the scientific method the best means of gaining knowledge, it provides the most effective tool known for dealing with the physical and social environment and promoting adaptive change. "[S]cience comes in to aid society in getting a method of progress" (Mead, 1936: 366).[9] It offers "the apparatus for the control over the environment and for bringing larger and larger ends and ideals within the vision of humanity" (Mead, 1936: 281). Applying a modified version of Darwin's theory of natural selection, Mead saw human societies as evolving and changing over time. "Societies develop, just as animal forms develop, by adjusting themselves to the problems that they find before them" (Mead, 1936: 365-366). Throughout most of history, evolution has taken place by relatively inefficient types of trial-and-error adjustment. "We look back over the history of plant and animal life on the face of the globe and see how [life] forms have developed slowly by the trial-and-error method" (Mead, 1936: 364). However, with the emergence of reflective intelligence and science, humans are learning to guide biological and social evolution in ways that are not as slow and wasteful as trial-and-error methods. Science provides "an instrument by means of which mankind, the community, gets control over its environment" (Mead, 1936: 360). Using Mead's examples, science allows us to control the types of crops we grow, the flow of rivers, population growth, and social reforms (Mead, 1899; 1936: 261f). Various methods of producing desirable change are treated as "working hypotheses" to be tested empirically. "The highest criterion that we can present is that the hypothesis shall *work* in the complex of forces into which we introduce it" (Mead, 1899/1964: 3).

The scientific method allows us to hasten adaptive social change by criticial, reflective analysis of all available data, hence to avoid the time-consuming and wasteful trial-and-error evolutionary processes. "The scientific method ... is, after all, only the evolutionary process grown self-conscious" (Mead, 1936: 364). That is to say, the scientific method allows us to replace the slow trial-and-error method of natural selection with self-conscious empirical methods of selection. Using the best current data, we can consciously and critically select those policies, programs, and technologies that have the best chance of being adaptive, then carefully evaluate and improve on these as new data are collected. With repeated application of these procedures, both knowledge and practical techniques evolve to increasingly sophisticated levels. Conscious, reflective selection, based on quality data, produces adaptive change much faster than does natural—that is, trial-and-error—selection (Mead, 1936: 383f). Thus, science "is a technique which is simply doing consciously what takes place naturally in the evolution of [life] forms" (Mead, 1936: 371). "Reflective consciousness . . . puts our own thought and endeavor into the very process of evolution. . ." (Mead, 1899/1964: 5).

PROVISIONAL TRUTH

Mead explained that pragmatism—and science—can only produce provisional truths, not absolute truths or static, unchanging dogmas (Mead, 1929a; 1932). This contrasts sharply with the claims of most philosophical systems that are not based on the scientific method. Before the development of modern science, most philosophers had sought stable, unchanging truths to provide continuity and stability amidst the flux and flow of human experience. "For the Psalmist the only form of continuity that gave security was that of the Everlasting Hills and for the Greeks it was the Unchangeable Heavens" (Mead, 1929b/1964: 352).[10] The medieval philosophers yearned "to rest in the arms of finality. Whether idealist or realist or neo-Kantian phenomenalist, [the philosopher] seeks repose for his perturbed spirit in the everlasting arms of an absolute of one sort or another" (Mead, 1929a/1964: 324). Even the philosophies based on Newton's mechanical conception of the world "give a static sort of picture of the universe" (Mead, 1936: 291). Mead concluded that most earlier philosophers were merely rationalizing the habits and attitudes of their times, rather than testing their philosophical ideas empirically (Mead, 1929a). "These speculations did not touch the world of things within which men lived and moved and had their being. Things were not analyzed" (Mead, 1929a/1964: 322).

Before the development of pragmatism, few philosophers cared about testing their theories in the world where we live out our lives. Because the speculative philosophers either distrusted their perception of—or doubted the importance of—the physical world, their only test of truth was the logic and "inner coherence" of their theories (Mead, 1929a/1964: 339). Naturally, rationalizations based on logic alone tend to produce static worldviews, along with the illusion of unchanging, absolute "truth."

After the development of scientific theories of evolution and relativity, it became increasingly difficult for people to believe in static worldviews; and the ever-growing power of science made it harder to neglect empirical data (Mead, 1932; 1936). As theories of stellar, biological, and social evolution were proposed and received increasing empirical support in the late 1800s and early 1900s, it became increasingly obvious that the world was not static and that unchanging "truths" could not correctly describe our dynamic, evolving universe.

> The point of view which comes in with the scientific method implies that, so far as our experience is concerned, the world is always different. Each morning we open our eyes upon a different universe. Our intelligence is occupied with continued adjustment to these differences. That is what makes the interest in life. We are advancing constantly into a new universe. . . [Mead, 1936: 291].

Theories of relativity in physics and psychology (Mead, 1927b; 1932) further undermined the credibility of claims to absolute "truth." Both physical and psychological relativity demonstrate that people's descriptions of the world will be different when they view the world from different perspectives.

As a result, twentieth-century thinkers have become increasingly aware that both knowledge and truths should not be expected to be static or absolute. Since the world is always changing and each new time frame provides novel perspectives on the world (Mead, 1932; 1936), we need a method for gaining knowledge that is designed to track the constant emergence of novel, unpredictable experience. The scientific method provides precisely that method (Mead, 1929b; 1932; 1936).

Every scientific theory is always open to change, and scientists are always searching for new data and theories. Using the example of the theory of infectious diseases, Mead stated:

> The scientist accepts this theory for the time being, but only as a postulate. He does not accept it as something to be taken in a dogmatic fashion. ... He is perfectly ready to find problems in all phases of his theory. In fact, the research scientist is looking for problems, and he feels happiest when he finds new ones. He does not cherish laws and the form in which they are given as something which must be maintained, something that must not be touched. On the contrary, he is anxious to find some exception to the statement of laws which has been given [Mead, 1936: 265].

"The scientist's procedure and method ... contemplate continued reconstruction in the face of events emerging in ceaseless novelty"

(Mead, 1932: 101-102). For Mead, the scientist's world is but a "working hypothesis" (Mead, 1929a/1964: 332). "The postulates of science are not dogmas..." (Mead, 1936: 259).

> And the scientist himself expects this [scientific] doctrine to be reconstructed just as other scientific doctrines have been reconstructed. He is confident that any later theory will assimilate into its relational structure the data of present-day science—in so far as these stand the test of repetition and improved technique [Mead, 1932: 105].

The openness of science and the scientist's interest in novel events makes science well-suited for the study and interpretation of a constantly changing and evolving universe.

Whereas dogmatic belief systems offer unchanging "truths" and a static worldview, science continually discovers new facts and demonstrates new theories (Mead, 1936: 288-291). "You can immediately see that this attitude involves a different view of the universe from that which is presented by dogmatic disciplines" (Mead, 1936: 290). "If we abandon one hypothesis, we at once set about to build up another. From the point of view of dogma, this procedure would be a confession of failure" (Mead, 1936: 289). But for Mead, the real failure lies in expecting absolute truth in a world of flux. "The immutable and incorruptible heavens exist only in rhetoric" (Mead, 1929b/1964: 352).

Mead argued that not only are provisional truths more accurate than absolute "truths," they are better suited for producing adaptive social change—that is, serving as tools of social reform (Mead, 1899; 1936). "Every attempt to direct conduct by a fixed idea of the world of the future must be, not only a failure, but also pernicious" (Mead, 1899/1964: 5). Because the world is always changing and evolving, ideas of fixed and absolute revealed truths are misleading: They promise beautiful, idealized solutions, but they do not provide tools for designing and adjusting social policies to stay in synchrony with the ever-changing world. They tend to be highly conservative and highly ideal (Mead, 1923/1964: 260-262). Chapters 9 and 10 explain Mead's defense of science as the best method for adjusting and reforming society to cope with the continual changes of the present world.

Given his thorough understanding of symbolic knowledge (see Chapter 6), Mead was fully aware that the hypotheses, principles, and laws of science are merely symbolic—verbal or mathematical—accounts about the world we experience (Mead, 1917a; 1932; 1936: 243-291, 326-378, 405-417). Scientific accounts are similar to all other accounts that we make about our world *except* that they are tested more rigorously than most other accounts (Mead, 1932: 9-31). In everyday life, people freely create accounts about their world; but many of these accounts would not receive strong empirical support.

Scientific accounts gain credibility only after they are tested repeatedly and demonstrate their usefulness. And even the most reliable of scientific accounts are accepted only as provisional truths, always open to reconstruction as new data and unexpected events emerge (Mead, 1929a; 1929b; 1932; 1934: 198, 329; 1936: 281-291).

Although Mead argued that science reflected the highest form of intelligence and he was basically optimistic that the continued use of science offered the best means of dealing with social problems, he could offer no promise about the future. "It is impossible to so forecast any future condition that depends upon the evolution of society as to be able to govern our conduct by such a forecast. It is always the unexpected that happens...and no human foresight is equal to this" (Mead, 1899/1964: 3). When facing problems, the scientific thinker "does not know what the solution will be, but he does know the method of the solution. We, none of us, know where we are going, but we do know that we are on the way" (Mead, 1923/1964: 266). "You see this is an advance in which we cannot state the goal toward which we are going" (Mead, 1936: 363). "It is a great secular adventure, that has reached some measure of success, but is still far from accomplishment" (Mead, 1923/1964: 265).

* * *

Pragmatism is a distinctively American form of philosophy (Mead, 1929-30). Having developed in the New World, it was free of some of the prescientific, metaphysical baggage that burdens most European philosophies. It is rooted in a "rough-and-ready" American ethic developed by the settlers who had faced the challenges of new frontiers and dealt with the practical problems of taming a new land. Pragmatism emerged at the time when evolution and other scientific theories were offering striking new views of the place of humans in the cosmos (Mead, 1923); and scientific research was providing practical solutions to ever-increasing numbers of problems (Mead, 1936). When the pragmatists demonstrated that the scientific method could resolve all the metaphysical problems that originated from idealistic models of some unknowable, preexistent reality, they could forget those useless mind games and turn to more important problems and more practical issues. Mead expressed a "sense of enormous relief" when escaping "that despairing sense of the philosophic Sisyphus vainly striving to roll the heavily weighted world of his reflection up into a preexistent reality" and turning "toward the future and join in the scientist's adventure" (Mead, 1929-30/1964: 389-390).

3

Mead's Unified Worldview

At numerous points in Mead's published work there is evidence that he organized his scientific and philosophical thought in terms of a unified empirical worldview. Two main strands of his writing bear on the topic. First, he advocated analyzing all ideas via the scientific method, thereby bringing all realms of knowledge into one organized scientific worldview—an empirical cosmology. Second, Mead was strongly opposed to mind-body dualism in all its forms because it split the world into two irreconcilable parts; and he succeeded in developing a nondualistic theory that unifies mind and body, mental and physical, subjective and objective. This chapter summarizes the evidence that Mead used an empirical cosmology to integrate and unify all knowledge in one internally consistent model.

MEAD'S SCIENTIFIC COSMOLOGY

Mead and the other pragmatists believed that the scientific method was the best method humans had ever developed for testing and advancing all forms of knowledge (Mead, 1917a; 1932; 1936; Dewey, 1916; 1938). By extending scientific inquiry to deal with the entire realm of human thought, they built the beginnings of a unified worldview that stated all knowledge in one common empirical language. Rather than splitting the world into separate studies—the sciences and humanities, or the *Natur-* and *Geisteswissenschaften*—the pragmatists attempted to evaluate all ideas empirically and organize the entire range of human knowledge in one well-integrated empirical cosmology.

The term "empirical cosmology" is being used to make clear that the pragmatic cosmology was significantly different from cosmologies based on contemplation and idealistic assumptions. Traditional philosophical cosmologies included nonempirical metaphysical assumptions that the pragmatists rejected because such ideas were untestable and unneeded. Mead (1900/1964: 9f; 1917a/1964: 201; 1924-25/1964: 269; 1932: 8f; 1936: 264f; 1938: 494-519) and other pragmatists (Morris, 1970: 110f) concluded that metaphysical problems were unnecessary "riddles" created by dualistic philosophies. Mead's psychological analysis of experience resolves all these metaphysical problems "and in so doing deprives the metaphysical system of its *raison d'être*" (Mead, 1900/1964: 10). Based solely on empirical methods, the pragmatist cosmology consists of a systematic organization of all currently available scientific knowledge, without any metaphysical assumptions.

The scientific method automatically builds toward a unified body of knowledge. The scientist is not satisfied with merely collecting data: "His impulse is not satisfied until the data have taken on the form of things in some sort of an ordered whole" (Mead, 1932: 94). Whenever two or more pieces of scientific information cannot be reconciled in a unified whole, they produce intellectual problems; and it is precisely such problems that Mead saw as the key motive that prompts scientists to develop new hypotheses and theories designed to resolve the problems (Mead, 1917a; 1932). "The scientist is continually noting that which departs from the accepted view, the given laws. With him it is not a disappointment but an achievement, a new problem to work on" (Mead, 1936: 282). Thus, any lack of unity in scientific data and theories presents the type of problem that leads to creative efforts to solve the problem and bring unity to the relevant data and theories. With repeated application of the scientific method, increasing amounts of data and theory are reconciled with each other in terms of ever broader and more all-inclusive theories. "Every new theory must take up into itself earlier doctrines and rationalize the earlier exceptions" (Mead, 1917a/1964: 204). By applying the same scientific method and scientific criteria to all facets of the cosmos, the pragmatists built the beginnings of a unified overview of all empirical knowledge—that is, an empirical cosmology.

The pragmatists did not expect that science or the empirical cosmology would ever reach a static, complete, and finalized form. Because we live in an ever-changing and evolving world in which new and unexpected data are always emerging, Mead anticipated that scientific knowledge would always be changing and evolving (Mead, 1917a; 1932). As new problems continually arise in every science, scientific theories are continually being rewritten and reconstructed; and there is no expectation of "approaching nearer and nearer toward a reality which would never change if it could be attained..." (Mead, 1917a/1964: 204). Because it is based on an ever-changing body of scientific knowledge, an empirical cosmology is always a "working hypothesis," a "provisional reality," open to further elaboration, adjustment, and refinement (Mead, 1929a/1964: 332; 1932: 95). "What is the world but a continued working hypothesis, a thought structure which is continually completing itself, as the problem breaks out now here and now there?" (Mead, 1929a/1964: 332).

Thus, science is a problem-solving system that works toward unity, without expecting to reach a final static state. Even though science can never provide complete or absolute truths, the empirical cosmology of our day is more comprehensive and powerful than any other world view has ever been. It provides a fairly well-unified view of almost all things from the history of the entire expanding universe down to the structure of the tiniest subatomic entities, from the oldest of life forms and civilizations down through their most recent scions.

Mead's interest in a unified scientific cosmology can be seen in other ways. In his essay, "A Pragmatic Theory of Truth," Mead explained how pragmatists can advance toward "seeing the world whole," while acknowledging the tentative, provisional nature of such a global overview (Mead, 1929a). The ability to see the world whole arises as a social product, as an individual gains increasing experience and symbolic knowledge.

> Seeing the world whole is response in the widest scope of such common [social] conduct. It means entering into the most highly organized logical, ethical, and aesthetic attitudes of the community...... ...Seeing the world whole is the recognition of the most extensive set of interwoven conditions that may determine thought, practice, and our fixation and enjoyment of values [Mead, 1929a/1964: 337].

For the thinking person, increasing amounts of life experience and reflective thought lead to an ever better grasp of the whole of human experience: "Can we not fairly say, that what we call our conscious life turns out to be one concatenated enterprise of thought, within which we become now intermittently and now steadily aware of the interwoven tissue of our seemingly discrete problems?" (Mead, 1929a/1964: 331). Although many people may go through life without becoming increasingly aware of the interwoven fabric of their different thoughts and problems, Mead's words suggest that his own thoughts were moving toward an ever-clearer conception of the world whole.

Mead recognized the complexity of the task of splicing together the myriad components of an all-inclusive worldview (Mead, 1900; 1906; 1929a). "The whole world of knowledge ... is an organic whole in which no necessary part can be changed without involving all the rest" (Mead, 1900/1964: 12). Because all knowledge is linked in an organic system, an advance in any one area can force a rethinking of other areas, thereby affecting the structure of the whole. Of course, the same holds true for science. "Science is, from an important point of view, a single body of knowledge, whose different parts determine each other mutually, though this mutual influence is often overlooked" (Mead, 1906/1964: 67). The organic interconnections are often overlooked by specialists who focus only on a small set of problems at a time; however, when specialists take the broader philosophical perspective, they can become concerned with the larger problems of linking all knowledge into an integrated system (Mead, 1932: 110f).

Although attempting to grasp the world as a whole is difficult—and never done with complete success—it is an essential intellectual undertaking when one recognizes the interconnectedness of all knowledge.

> Is it not true that the solution of no one problem can be achieved without that of many others and perhaps without the solution of all of them? This is beyond doubt what we are apt to imply when we undertake to grasp the world as a whole, and bring into vital unity the presentations of many sciences, and get out to our view the involvements of each in each other. It is genuine thinking because it leaves nothing out [Mead, 1929a/1964: 331].

Even though genuine thinking that leaves nothing out is essential for understanding the interconnectedness of all knowledge, Mead stated that he anticipated only "partial solutions" (Mead, 1929a/1964: 332) and that he was not being swept "into the current of Idealism"—with its illusions of moving toward truth "at infinity" (Mead, 1917a/1964: 204). Mead expected his knowledge to be imperfect and ephemeral.

> And we know that our children will inhabit a different world from ours and will inevitably rewrite the annals we have so laboriously composed. But this does not disturb us, nor do we feel that seeing our world whole involves the vision of their future.... ...Seeing the world whole is gathering that import [of the fathomless wealth of the perceptual present] so far as in us lies [Mead, 1929a/1964: 335].

In Mead's essay on the importance of teaching natural science at the college level (Mead, 1906), we can see that he sincerely hoped that many people—even those who were not scientists—could be given a chance to see the scientific view of the world whole. He suggested ways for improving college education in the natural sciences in order to help students "grasp the most important achievements in modern thought" (Mead, 1906/1964: 61). He regretted the fact "that the natural sciences are not interconnected in the minds of the students, that they exist in watertight compartments" (Mead, 1906/1964: 64), and he presented practical suggestions for helping students see the broad overview of science and its view of the world as a whole.

One of Mead's suggestions was to teach science through the history of scientific development. "The interdependence of scientific effort and achievement, and the interrelationship which exists between all science in presenting its world as a whole, can be brought out vividly only when its history is being presented..." (Mead, 1906/1964: 67). The historical approach helps students see how science was a natural development of human inquiry. It also helps them see "the relations which have subsisted between scientific investigation and the whole field of human endeavor ... its relation to commerce, industry, the geographical distribution of men, their interconnection with each other, and the other sides of their intellectual life. Science would be interwoven with the whole human world of which it is actually a part" (Mead, 1906/1964: 66). Mead suggested that students can best learn science when the particulars are seen in the context of the larger whole. "It is good educational doctrine that the whole is more concrete than the part" (Mead, 1906/1964: 68). Once students grasp the whole overview, it is easy for them to see the importance and relevance of each part. Therefore science instructors who wish to help the student should "present the part to him by means of the whole" (Mead, 1906/1964: 69). For example, "it is a great deal easier to present the problem of evolution in the world as a whole than it is in the specific instance" (Mead, 1906/1964: 68).

Even for the student of the humanities, the scientific view of the cosmos is relevant. "Science is responsible for the view of the universe as a whole which must be the background for our theology as well as our philosophy and much that is finest in our literature" (Mead, 1906/1964: 71). In addition, Mead noted that scholars in the humanities were increasingly using the scientific method for studying "languages, history, literature and the so-called social sciences" (Mead, 1906/1964: 61), hence students in the humanities also needed to learn the scientific method.

Mead concluded his article on science education with an emphasis on unity: "Science faculties ... should so organize the courses which their students take, that they will get the unity which every college course ought to give." "It is requisite at the end as at the beginning that the student should see his world as a whole..." (Mead, 1906/1964: 72).

Clearly, Mead believed that both at the beginning of years of study and at the end, an overview of the unity of all knowledge is valuable.

Mead himself had learned much about the unity of all scientific knowledge through studying the history of science, and he was quite knowledgeable about the topic. He wrote extensively on the history of science, presenting beautifully detailed histories of science from ancient Greece and Renaissance times through his own period (Mead, 1917a; 1932; 1936). His detailed knowledge of Greek science helped him display its inadequacies and thereby emphasize the strengths of modern experimental science (Mead, 1917a). His knowledge of Darwin's and Pasteur's biographical accounts of their own scientific discoveries provided Mead with the foundations for his criticisms of positivism and for the development of the pragmatic philosophy of science (Mead, 1917a/1964: 190f; 1932). Mead interwove theories of relativity, stellar evolution, biological evolution, and the evolution of consciousness to create a unified empirical theory of emergence (Mead, 1932). Mead traced the history of ideas—especially those involving science—that shaped nineteenth-century philosophical thought (Mead, 1936). These and other writings reveal that Mead had organized an enormous range of the history of science and philosophy into a meaningful whole.

Naturally, Mead's unified and organic worldview included society, too. For example, he placed his micro social theories within the context of the social whole: "For social psychology, the whole (society) is prior to the part (the individual), not the part to the whole" (Mead, 1934: 7). In his lectures on the evolution of science, Mead traced the history of scientific and social theories and noted their common themes: "It is very interesting to see the sources from which importantly constructive ideas have arisen, to see what an organic thing society is; how ideas that you find in one phase of it appear in some different form in another phase, but come back to common sources" (Mead, 1936: 245).

Although some people recoil from the empirical cosmology when they see the humble position that it accords to humans, Mead did not. Mead summarized Huxley's view of "physical science, that sees in the whole life of the human race but an inconsiderable moment on an inconsiderable speck within the physical universe, that finds in a civilized moral society an aberration from a biological nature that is red in tooth and claw, and subject to a ruthless law of the survival of the fittest" (Mead, 1923/1964: 250). Mead's only exception to this was that he took a somewhat more benign view of evolution, because evolution clearly allows for the emergence of altruism and social cooperation (Mead, 1923/1964: 251). In fact, through their cooperative efforts, scientists have amassed an enormous wealth of information that not only shows us how inconsequential we are but also gives us unprecedented amounts of knowledge and power:

> The physical universe which by its enormity has crushed the human insect into disappearing insignificance has ... shown itself infinitely complaisant in magnifying man's mechanical capacity. In accepting his negligible crevice in the physical whole man has found access to the minute structure of things and by this route has reached both the storehouse and powerhouse of nature. ... If humanity has fled shivering from the starry spaces, it has become minutely at home in the interstices of the speck that it inhabits for an instant [Mead, 1923/1964: 253].

"Not only is man as an animal and as an inquirer into nature at home in the world, but the society of men is equally a part of the order of the universe" (Mead, 1923/1964: 264).

Throughout the remainder of this book, we will see further evidence that Mead thought in terms of a unified scientific worldview. He wrote extensively on the problems of dualism and created a nondual model that unifies mind and body, mental and physical, objective and subjective (see next section). Mead's method of inquiry was designed to unify all scientific knowledge in terms of process (see Chapter 4). And the overview of his theories, presented in Chapters 5 through 10, shows that all the parts of his published work and lectures fit together nicely in one unified system. Mead came close to being a modern-day Renaissance man: He succeeded in integrating an enormous range of ideas from many areas of the sciences and the humanities in terms of one internally consistent empirical cosmology.

BEYOND DUALISM

In applying the scientific and evolutionary perspective to psychology and philosophy, Mead and Dewey concluded that the traditional dualistic model of mind and body was untenable (Mead, 1927b; 1929-30). Traditional theories had dealt with mind and body separately, thus splitting the world into two parts: mental and physical. In the past, this bifurcation of the world into subjective and objective has been one of the major impediments to the development of a unified worldview. Mead and Dewey demonstrated that a scientific, evolutionary analysis of mind and body would produce a nondualistic cosmology in which all facets of the human condition—mental and physical, subjective and objective—could be dealt with in one unified model. A brief look at Mead's analysis of the mind-body problem will further demonstrate how deep his commitment was to building a unified empirical cosmology.

Mead traced the traditional belief in mind-body dualism to the idealistic philosophies that were common before the development of modern scientific and evolutionary thinking (Mead, 1917a; 1927a; 1929-30; 1936). In order to attain a sense of stable, everlasting truth in a world of flux and change, Plato divided the world into two parts: the ever-changing reality of our immediate senses, and an eternal, unchanging reality of pure, static "ideal essence ... seen in a world beyond the heavens" (Mead, 1917a/1964: 171). According to the ancient Greek dualistic cosmology, our bodies were part of the "world of imperfectly developed matter" (Mead, 1917a/1964: 182); but our minds and souls could transcend to the higher, eternal realm of perfect and absolute truth. Early Christian theologians adopted a modified version of the Platonic model, with its dualistic conceptualization of body and soul. Again the body was tied to the finite earth—cycling from "ashes to ashes, dust to dust"—while the soul was given "sure and certain hope of ... eternal life" (*The Book of Common Prayer: Burial of the Dead,* 1928: 333).

In the seventeenth century, Descartes developed another variation on mind-body dualism. "For Descartes, mind and body were distinct substances neither of which depended upon the other for its being" (Mead, 1936: 307). Descartes reached this conclusion after questioning whether there is any knowledge that is beyond all doubt. After a critical analysis of all ideas obtained from the body's five senses and from the workings of the mind, he decided that the only thing he could know for certain—without any doubts—was that he was doubting, that he was thinking. From this position of extreme skepticism, he concluded that the only *sure* knowledge that we can have is that we are thinking, and that thinking is indubitable proof of our existence: "I think, therefore I am." Even early scientists adopted a form of mind-body dualism. "Not even the English empiricists saw the [mind-body] problem in terms of a functional relationship. Their psychology ... undertook to give a statement of the structure of things [as perceived] which at the same time left things 'out there'" (Mead, 1936: 307). By retaining a clear distinction between the "subjective" and "objective" world and failing to explain the functional relationship between them, they perpetuated a dualistic worldview.

Given the almost universal acceptance of mind-body dualism, it seemed natural for early psychologists to use introspection—turning inward to investigate subjective experience—as a primary method for obtaining knowledge about human thought and action. If one assumes that mind and body are made of separate "substances" and that subjective experience is more reliable than the objective information based on the five senses, it is easy to conclude that the subjective, introspective approach to psychology—if not to everything else—is more appropriate than an objective, empirical approach.

Mead and Dewey took the opposite view, rejecting the dualistic assumption that mind consists of some special substance. "The postulate of mind as the locus of a spiritual protoplasm is unwarranted" (Mead, 1927a: 121). The pragmatists recognized that mind-body dualism was one of the greatest impediments to the construction of unified theories of the world because it requires two separate languages for treating the two separate substances of mind and body. These separate languages create unresolvable problems if you *assume* that mind and body—subjective and objective—cannot be united. Mead objected to this: "We do not want two languages, one of certain physical facts and one of certain conscious facts." Otherwise, ... "the head you talk about is not stated in terms of the head you are observing" (Mead, 1934: 40). Instead, Mead sought to "bring these two phases of the experience as close to each other as possible, or translate them into language which is common to both fields" (Mead, 1934: 40).

As a first step toward overcoming dualism, Mead adopted an objective language that described private, mental processes in the same terms as publicly observable conversation: "Thinking is the same as talking to other people" (Mead, 1927a: 155), except that it is done inwardly, with oneself rather than with others. "The mechanism of thinking [is] that of inward conversation" (Mead, 1932: 84). Mead traced the development of this "inward conversation" as it emerges in childhood (Mead, 1912; 1934): As the child learns to talk with others, the child gains the ability to talk with self. "The child will converse for hours with himself, even constructing imaginary companions, who function in the child's growing self-consciousness as the processes of inner speech—of thought and imagination—function in the consciousness of the adult" (Mead, 1912/1964: 137). By adulthood, "the features and intonations of the dramatis personae fade out and the emphasis falls upon the meaning of the inner speech, the imagery becomes merely the barely necessary cues" (Mead, 1913/1964: 147). However, at all ages, "the very process of thinking is, of course, simply an inner conversation. . ." (Mead, 1934: 141). "[I]t is this inner thought, this inner flow of speech and what it means ... that ... constitutes the mind..." (Mead, 1936: 381).

The next question, then, is how best to study talking and the inner conversation that is called mind. By the late 1800s, the power of Darwin's evolutionary theory and the success of science in producing reliable knowledge about the physical world were leading many psychologists—and some philosophers—to approach all facets of animal and human behavior from the evolutionary point of view. Instead of assuming that "I think, therefore I am," Mead took the evolutionary viewpoint: We think because we have evolved as social animals with the capacity for symbolic communication, thus with the ability to speak and think symbolically (Mead, 1929a/1964: 342). Rather than assuming the primacy of the mind (as Descartes had), Mead explained how mind emerged during biological and social evolution (Mead, 1909; 1914: 31f; 1924-25; 1932: 68f; 1934: 42f). Comparing insects, lower vertebrates, and advanced species, Mead traced the gradual appearance of increasingly complex central nervous systems, increasingly subtle communicative gestures, and eventually symbolic vocal gestures (Mead, 1924-25/1964: 278f). Only when people began to use language for symbolic social interaction did mind and self emerge as private internal conversations in the head (Mead, 1910c; 1912). In discussing the emergence of consciousness, Mead stated: "In evolution not only have new [life] forms appeared, but new qualities or contents in [conscious] experience." "And these new characters and new meanings exist in nature as do the forms of physical objects..." (Mead, 1924-25/1964: 273). It is important to notice Mead's nondualistic stance that the emergence of higher levels of consciousness occur *in nature;* they do not rise above nature to a transcendental reality, to a Platonic heaven, or to the status of a special substance. "If mind is simply an emergent character of certain organisms in their so-called intelligent responses to their environment, mind can never transcend the environment within which is operates" (Mead, 1932: 118).

Mead stressed that biological evolution only provides part of the nondualistic explanation of mind. Biology explains the human potential for symbolic interaction and mind; but verbal socialization is needed for the actualization of that biological potential. People must live in groups, learn language, and talk with others before they can talk with themselves in the inner conversation of the mind.

> The human being's physiological capacity for developing mind or intelligence is a product of the process of biological evolution, just as is his whole organism; but the actual development of his mind or intelligence itself, given that capacity, must proceed in terms of the social situations wherein it gets its expression and import; and hence it itself is a product of the process of social evolution, the process of social experience and behavior [Mead, 1934: 226].

At various places, Mead discussed how vocal gestures and significant symbols emerged in social evolution, thereby making possible both public speech and private inner thought (Mead, 1912; 1924-25; 1927a; 1934). "This mental process, then, is one which has evolved in the social process of which it is a part" (Mead, 1936: 381).

One reason evolutionary theories played such an important role in the pragmatists' work is that evolution provided a means for unifying mind and body. For Dewey (as well as for James before him), "it was biological science with its dominant conception of evolution that offered him a process within which to analyze and place intelligence" (Mead, 1929-30/1964: 387). Viewing the emergence of mind and body in the broad sweep of biological and social evolution allowed the pragmatists to locate the functional relations between mind and body as these two evolved together. From the evolutionary perspective, it was easy to see mind as part of the whole of nature—as one of the many complex natural things that have arisen through evolutionary processes (Mead, 1932: 68-90).

Mead described his efforts to place mind and subjective things back in their proper place in nature in terms of returning stolen goods (Mead, 1927a: 154; also see Mead, 1927a: 106; 1927b/1964: 306, 315). "The philosophical value of this position is that it restores stolen goods to the world" (Mead, 1927a: 154). Mead accused the dualistic philosophers of stealing mind and subjective things from nature and placing them in a separate world—as a special "substance"—that was presumed to be different from the world of bodily and earthly things. Dualistic "philosophy had stolen [subjective] qualities and meaning from the world and placed them in a mind that is entirely suppositious, and then abandoned the task of getting from this mind to other minds and to the world" (Mead, 1927a: 154). By abandoning the task of connecting the thinker's mind with other minds and with the natural world, dualist philosophers created two serious problems: (1) solipsism and (2) the impossibility of establishing a functional relationship between the mind and the world (i.e., "getting from this mind [1] to other minds and [2] to the world"). Mead objected to both of these.

First, dualism leads to solipsism—the belief that the mind or self can know nothing outside of itself. "Each self is an island, and each self is sure only of its own island, for who knows what mirages may arise above this analogical sea" (Mead, 1910a/1964: 107). If we agree with Descartes that our only sure knowledge is that we are thinking, we leave each individual hopelessly stranded inside his or her own head, unable to see the world from the perspective of other people, unable to know what other minds are thinking. "It meant that the real world had to be translated into the perspective of each one [each individual], and that there was no way of getting out of one's perspective into that of somebody else." Solipsism " . . . means the defeat by any universal philosophy or, seemingly, of science" (Mead, 1936: 413). From the solipsistic point of view, a person's philosophy or science can include only the analysis of that single individual's limited subjective world.

The problems of solipsism disappear once we realize that each individual's thoughts and self emerge only through social interaction. "What I want particularly to emphasize is the temporal and logical pre-existence of the social process to the self-conscious individual that arises in it" (Mead, 1934: 186). The child gains the internal conversation called mind only through symbolic interaction with other people. "There cannot be a solipsistic situation; there must be other selves" (Mead, 1927a: 162). In his renouncement of all individualistic theories of self, Mead stated that "mind can never find expression, and could never have come into existence at all, except in terms of a social environment..." (Mead, 1934: 223). Mead's social and evolutionary theory can explain the relation of one self to others, whereas solipsism (and individualistic philosophies in general) cannot. "Solipsism is an absurdity. The self has reality only as other selves have reality, and comes in fact later" (Mead, 1914: 55). Commenting on the introspective view, Mead stated: "The old view held that the self could be directly consciousness of itself..." [This] "is not true. The self cannot arise in experience except as there are others there" (Mead, 1927a: 155-156).

Second, Mead objected to the dualistic view that mind was separate from nature and not capable of being functionally related to the body and the environment. Rather than separating mind from nature, Mead stated that "we can ... restore to nature all that a dualistic doctrine has relegated to consciousness..." (Mead, 1927b/1964: 315). "We must get rid of the bifurcation of the world and restore to nature or the objective order what belongs to it" (Mead, 1927a: 107). Once mind is returned to its rightful place in the body (which in turn is located in its social and physical environment), it is clear that it can be studied naturalistically, using the objective methods of the natural sciences (Mead, 1900; 1924-25; 1927a; 1936). Objective psychology's "sympathies have always been with the presuppositions and method of the natural sciences" (Mead, 1924-25/1964: 269). "Mind and body are not to be separated on the basis of our present physical science" (Mead, 1927a: 167).

The scientific psychologies that arose to replace introspective psychology at the end of the nineteenth century abolished dualism by establishing a functional relationship between mind and body, inside and outside events.

> The mind is no longer something here, something inside, which gets impressions from something there, something outside. The inner and the outer, the subjective and the objective, are phases of a single process and point to differences of perspective, not to absolute differences of locus. ... Just as there is a functional relationship between the organism and its environment, so there is one between what is "in the mind" and what is "outside" [Mead, 1936: 307].

"We must consider inside and outside together, and the world cannot be divided into inside and outside" (Mead, 1927a: 107). Mead's own social psychology succeeded in unifying mind and body, mental and physical, objective and subjective, inside and outside in one non-dualistic model (see Chapters 5-8).

Although some thinkers could entertain the extreme skepticism that led Descartes to his totally subjective and solipsistic view, "for no modern scientists has skepticism been a practical problem" (Mead, 1929-30/1964: 379). "Science itself has never been disturbed by this sort of so-called 'subjective idealism'" (Mead, 1936: 413). The world we all experience every day—no matter what it may be in actuality—is to be taken seriously and studied scientifically (Mead, 1932). "I take it that the most distinctive mark of the pragmatic movement is the frank acceptance of actual ongoing experience, experimentally controlled, as the standpoint from which to interpret the past and anticipate the future" (Mead, 1929a/1964: 344).

Using social evolutionary theories and the scientific method to return mind to the body and the natural order of the cosmos, Mead removed one of the most serious obstacles to developing a unified empirical cosmology. Whereas some contemporary sociologists still have not been able to solve the perplexing metaphysical problems created by the bifurcation of the world into two separate substances—mind and body—Mead resolved the metaphysical problems and dissolved the split: "The solution of the problem carries with it the disappearance of the problem and the metaphysical system at the same time" (Mead, 1900/1964: 10).

Toward the end of his life, Mead described "the dualism of mind and nature" as "becoming every day more intolerable" (Mead, 1927b/1964: 307). Among his last works, he utilized theories of evolution, relativity, and social psychology to argue for the unity and continuity of things that on the surface appear to be dual (Mead, 1927a; 1929b; 1932).

* * *

This chapter has presented evidence that Mead thought in terms of a unified empirical cosmology and that he strongly opposed the dualistic separation of mind and body, mental and physical, objective and subjective. Subsequent chapters demonstrate that when we follow Mead's method his written works and lecture material fit together neatly in one unified system.

4

Mead's Methods

We have seen that Mead organized and unified his thoughts in terms of an empirical cosmology. The next task is to determine *how* he organized and constructed his specific intellectual system. Many scientists develop an empirical worldview, but each is likely to approach the task differently. For example, we would expect a physicist to develop a different worldview than would a chemist or biologist. The empirical worldview of a psychologist or sociologist would be still different. In fact, within any given discipline, each individual would construct a different synthesis of the available empirical data, depending on his or her own unique interests and perspectives on the discipline (Mead, 1924-25/1964: 276; 1936: 415f).

Given the difficulties of grasping the world whole (Mead, 1929a), it is to be expected that any scientist's empirical cosmology will have limitations. Therefore, it is no surprise that Mead's unified theory overrepresented some topics and underrepresented others. Mead's primary focus was on social processes, showing the unity and interaction of the mental and physical components involved in micro and macro social phenomena. His secondary focus was on the network of reciprocal relations between the individual, the society, and the larger environmental systems. Although the emphasis of Mead's unified theory might not be of great interest to physicists and chemists, it is quite relevant to micro and macro sociologists, psychologists, and philosophers.

Although Mead never brought all his ideas together in one grand synthesis, he left two types of information that allow us to reconstruct a summary of his unified worldview. First, he wrote and lectured on a large number of topics, providing us with well-developed statements of his ideas on a broad range of subjects. Second, his work contains numerous examples of the methods he used for synthesizing material from various levels—on biology, psychology, micro and macro societal phenomena, and broader ecological issues. It is these methods that can help us assemble Mead's diverse ideas in the same manner that he did, thereby producing a unified theory that should resemble his own. Naturally, our reconstruction[11] will be incomplete because we cannot include those thoughts that Mead did not commit to writing or that were not in lectures for which we have reliable student notes.

Throughout the remaining chapters we will draw on Mead's writings and the notes from his lectures for information about his specific ideas and his methods for weaving those ideas into an integrated whole. Highest priority will be given to the written works that Mead published during his own life, because we are most confident that these writings accurately represent his own views. Second priority will be given to unpublished works and the student notes taken during his lectures, as these may not be as well formulated or accurately recorded as Mead would have wished. The contents of unpublished work and student notes will not be used if they contradict or are not compatible with the work Mead published during his life. To avoid producing too narrow a picture of Mead's unified theory, as much of Mead's work will be used as is possible.

This chapter summarizes Mead's methods, and the following chapters utilize these methods to assemble his ideas in an internally consistent, unified theory. The major features of Mead's methods derive from his stance as a process philosopher and from his commitment to objective, scientific methods for the study of human conduct.

PROCESS PHILOSOPHY

A central theme of Mead's writing is that the world of knowledge is an organic whole, in which all the parts affect each other to produce a dynamically fluctuating system (Mead, 1900; 1906; 1929a; 1932). What is the best strategy for approaching the study of a complex and constantly changing organic whole? What methods are best suited for describing such systems without creating static, compartmentalized models? An examination of Mead's writings and lectures reveals that his key method of approach was to organize all topics in terms of evolutionary processes, developmental processes, interactional processes, and other types of processes. For this reason, Mead has been described as a "process philosopher." As Miller pointed out, "This meant for him that the temporal dimension cannot be excluded from the real; the real is not timeless but consists of acts, happenings, or events'' (Miller, 1982: 4). Thus, one component of Mead's methods is a focus on process, viewing all elements of the complex organic whole as they interact and change over time. Social scientists who follow this method could never produce static structural theories or idealized systems, like those created by Talcott Parsons.

Mead's most general method of approach to any problem was to locate it within all relevant processes—be they evolutionary, historical, developmental, socialization, interactional, mental, or any other. A review of his writings shows that he organized the different types of processes within a two-phase cycle[12] which (1) worked down from the macro level (e.g., evolutionary and historical processes) to the micro level (e.g., behavioral and mental processes), then (2) worked back up to macro level (e.g., social and ecological processes). This two-phase method allowed Mead to deal with all types of processes in ways that revealed the effects of macro processes on micro as well as micro processes on macro. An attempt to organize all the processes in terms of either phase by itself would do injustice to the other, creating the erroneous impression that one of the levels (either macro or micro) was of predominant importance. The use of a two-phase cycle helped Mead explain the reciprocal influences of macro and micro.

In the first phase, Mead used evolutionary processes to trace the origin of the universe, life on earth, the human species, and human societies. The larger systems of stellar and planetary evolution set the stage for the process of biological evolution on earth (Mead, 1932: 47ff; 1936: 348ff). Mead gave considerable attention to the process of biological evolution and the emergence of animals with increasingly complex nervous systems and behavioral capacities (Mead, 1907; 1924-1925; 1932: 68ff; 1936: 364f). Next he dealt with the processes of social evolution. He was especially concerned with the evolution of early human social interaction and the origins of vocal gestures, because these made possible the emergence of language, symbolic interaction, and symbolic mental processes (Mead, 1909; 1910c; 1912; 1914; 1934). At various points, Mead dealt with social evolution, sometimes referring to the social structure, interaction patterns, and socialization processes of primitive peoples (Mead, 1906; 1910b; 1936). He traced the historical processes that produced ever more complex Western societies, and he commented on the trends he saw in the development of large, complex modern societies (Mead, 1914; 1924-25; 1929c; 1936).

In dealing with individuals located at any point of social evolution, Mead turned to the developmental and socialization processes to explain the origin of their conduct. Rather than treating adult behavior—such as social skills, language, and mental capabilities—as givens, Mead traced their development from infancy through childhood to the full adult form (Mead, 1914; 1922; 1934). He described the socialization process in considerable detail, dealing especially with parent-child interactions, the process by which the child acquires language, the role of children's play and games in training skills for symbolic interaction with others—and with oneself in the inner forum of the mind (Mead, 1912; 1924-25; 1927a; 1934). He showed how socialization processes influence the development of an increasingly structured self, reflective intelligence, and an organized conception of the world (Mead, 1913; 1934).

In the second phase, Mead worked back from the micro processes at the individual level to more macro processes, demonstrating how the individual's actions affect others and society. He showed how mental processes are used to solve problems in everyday life, moral decisions, science, and social reform (Mead, 1899; 1917a; 1923; 1929c; 1934; 1936). He dealt with social interaction, as it is mediated by role taking, sympathy, and reflective intelligence (Mead, 1912; 1914; 1936). He explained why the child focuses first on micro social relations and gradually gains skills for dealing with—and having increasing impact on—macro societal processes and the larger environment (Mead, 1923; 1929c; 1934; 1936). He dealt with the effects of the conduct of individuals and institutions on larger ecological processes, as people grapple with various environmental problems. It is here that Mead argued that science, as the highest development of reflective intelligence, was the best method we have for solving problems and guiding social evolution (Mead, 1936).

Mead's method of locating all events in their correct place in this two-phase cycle allowed him to do justice to both macro and micro processes and their reciprocal influences. This method also allowed him to weave all the components of his worldview into one dynamic whole. If we wish to reconstruct Mead's unified theory from his written work and lectures, we can utilize his methods and reconstruct the same general organization of ideas. Chapters 5 through 10 demonstrate how this is done and provide additional evidence that this is in fact the method Mead used to organize his thoughts into a unified whole.

Against Purely Mechanical Theories. Mead's position as a process philosopher can be clarified further by examining his opposition to purely mechanical theories that neglect process. To illustrate the differences between the two perspectives, Mead often used Newtonian mechanics as an example that contrasted with his process models (Mead, 1932: 32-46; 1936: 249-281). ''The Newtonian doctrine presented a picture of an orderly, mechanical universe, one governed by mechanical laws, a universe of masses in motion"(Mead, 1936: 251).

A traditional example from classical mechanics—the motion of billiard balls on a perfectly smooth, level, frictionless table—allows us to see Mead's point clearly. Once a billiard ball has been set in motion, it should stay in motion, traveling at the same speed and in the same direction, unless acted upon by some external object. This is the first law of thermodynamics: the conservation of energy. If the ball hits a second ball of equal mass, the angle and velocity of impact allow us to predict the exact velocity and trajectory of both balls after impact. Everything is predictable. Everything is perfectly determined. There is no room for the unknown or the unexpected. In such a mechanical system, novel and unanticipated events do not occur. "Seemingly, the whole world would be absolutely fixed and determined. That is a conceivable statement of this mechanical science" (Mead, 1936: 250).

Although Mead acknowledged that the mechanical model worked quite well in explaining the motion and transformation of inanimate objects (Mead, 1932: 34), he stated that it "did not deal with the characters which belong to living organisms" (Mead, 1936: 260). "Plants and animals ... present to science objects whose essential characters are found not in that which undergoes [mechanical] transformation but in the process itself..." (Mead, 1932: 34). Although mechanistic and deterministic principles may illuminate much of the inanimate world, Mead emphasized repeatedly that novel and unexpected things are continually arising in biological, behavioral, and social systems (Mead, 1899; 1929b; 1932; 1936). For example, in the biological realm, random mutations and novel recombinations of genetic information are essential for the evolution of new species. In a perfectly mechanical system, there would be no novel and unexpected variations in any given species, hence no possibility for change, evolution, or the emergence of new species.

Similarly in human conduct, it is the behavioral novelties that make change and social evolution possible. Although admitting the continuity of experience, Mead added, "There is a tang of novelty in each moment of experience." "The [novel] break reveals the continuity, while the continuity is the background for the novelty" (Mead, 1929b/1964: 350). "Our experience involves the continual appearance of that which is new. We are always advancing into a future which is different from the past" (Mead, 1936: 290). The novelties make it impossible to develop a fully mechanical, deterministic model of human life and social evolution. "It is impossible to so forecast any future condition that depends upon the evolution of society as to be able to govern our conduct by such a forecast. It is always the unexpected that happens . . . and no human foresight is equal to this" (Mead, 1899/ 1964: 3).

Inasmuch as the pragmatists avoided all metaphysical questions as inherently unanswerable, Mead did not ask if the world "really" is a deterministic system or not. He merely assumed that, practically speaking, humans would never know enough to predict everything, thus the unexpected would always occur. As Mead stated the problem:

> This brings out the general question as to whether anything novel can appear. Practically, of course, the novel is constantly happening and the recognition of this gets its expression in more general terms in the concept of emergence. Emergence involves a reorganization, but the reorganization brings in something that was not there before [Mead, 1934: 198].

Mead gave the example of the emergence of water, which has qualities that cannot be predicted from the qualities of the elements that constitute it. "Water is a combination of hydrogen and oxygen, but water was not there before in the separate elements" (Mead, 1934: 198).

Mead used examples from numerous types of processes to demonstrate that emergence is common in nature (Mead, 1932; 1936): stellar evolution, the evolution of the planets, the emergence of water, life, behavior, and consciousness. Because novel events are continually emerging, our methods should be geared to deal with such events. As discussed in Chapter 2, Mead considered science to be the best method for dealing with a constantly changing, evolving world, though he did not expect it to produce the finality of absolute truth (Mead, 1917a; 1929a; 1932; 1936). "The scientist's procedure and method contemplate no such finality. On the contrary, they contemplate continued reconstruction [of scientific theories] in the face of events emerging in ceaseless novelty" (Mead, 1932: 101-102). In fact, scientists look forward to the emergence of novel events as a source of new empirical problems (Mead, 1936: 281-284).

Mead pointed out that the Newtonian view of the world as a deterministic, mechanistic system was a *postulate*—not dogma (Mead, 1936: 270-278).[13] The postulate has worked so well in so many cases that scientists in the mechanical sciences typically approach problems—even those involving emergent events—with methods designed to create deterministic models. Speaking from the viewpoint of exact scientists, Mead said, "The emergent has no sooner appeared than we set about rationalizing it, that is, we undertake to show that it, or at least the conditions that determine its appearance, can be found in the past that lay behind it" (Mead, 1932: 14). "Whatever does happen, even the emergent, happens under determining conditions—especially, from the standpoint of the exact sciences..." (Mead, 1932: 15). However, Mead emphasized that no matter how precise the mechanical models become, "these conditions never determine completely the 'what it is' that will happen" (Mead, 1932: 15). Rather than totally rejecting mechanical science, Mead advocated integrating both mechanism and emergence into a larger theoretical framework. "It is the task of the philosophy of today to bring into congruence with each other this universality of determination which is the text of modern [mechanistic] science, and the emergence of the novel..." (Mead, 1932: 14).

Toward Balance. A second example from classical mechanics allows us to illuminate further the relationship between purely mechanical Newtonian models and Mead's views. The second law of thermodynamics states that during energy transformations—for example, whenever work is done—some energy is always wasted and lost, hence the total available energy in the system is always declining. The continual loss of energy is described in terms of entropy. The components of the Newtonian universe are moving, "as we have seen from the conception of entropy, toward a condition of stagnation" (Mead, 1936: 291): The universe is running downhill. However, Mead pointed out that living systems, in a certain sense, work against stagnation and entropy: They collect energy, organize it to higher levels of order and partially reverse the downhill flow of energy. In the physical sciences, "the theory of entropy regards nature as being on a hill and running down, but living forms differ from this inasmuch as they are able to work uphill, to reinstate a lost situation. Life breaks down but arises again; a higher form emerges from a single cell; the life process pushes forward and upward" (Mead, 1927a: 108).

Again we see that the assumptions of the mechanical sciences fail to do justice to the processes of living systems. Therefore the methods of the life sciences—including the behavioral and social sciences—need to be different from those of the purely mechanistic sciences.

For Mead, behavioral and social processes are to be seen as natural developments of the life process. Through evolutionary processes, both animal and human behavior are "calculated to maintain life under all conditions" (Mead, 1927a: 110). "Behavior thus goes back to the life process" (Mead, 1927a: 115). "The psychologist starts with life..." (Mead, 1927a: 116). Therefore, the methods used for studying behavior and society need to be more similar to those of biology than to those of the mechanistic sciences—physics and chemistry. "The difference between the physicist and the biologist evidently lies in the goals which their sciences contemplate, in the realities they are seeking. And their procedure answers to their goals" (Mead, 1932: 35). Physicists use reductionistic procedures, tearing larger structures down into their parts; whereas biologists use evolutionary or developmental processes to explain the production of ever more complex, self-organizing, purposive systems. The procedure "of the physical scientist is reduction and that of the biologist is production" (Mead, 1932: 35).

Mechanistic methods fail to identify all that is going on in life, behavior, and social processes. "In the purely mechanistic statement there is something left over, and this is a necessary consequence of the method of physical science" (Mead, 1927a: 110). To use one of Mead's examples (Mead, 1936: 268), the digestive system not only mechanically breaks down food, it has a function—a purpose—in maintaining life. An analysis that focused solely on the mechanical transformations of food would miss the function of the digestive system for sustaining life processes. "The complete mechanical statement would not take account of the end, of the purpose. . ." that is seen in living systems "and that seems to be necessary to our comprehension of the world" (Mead, 1936: 272).

Mead used the word "teleology" to describe the purposeful, life-sustaining processes that were overlooked by a purely mechanistic analysis of living systems (Mead, 1927a: 108ff; 1936: 268ff). However, he clearly dissociated himself from the nonscientific form of teleology espoused by vitalists.[14] Mead was highly critical of vitalists such as Bergson because they postulated the existence of vital forces and opposed scientific analysis of living things (Mead, 1936: 292-325). "Sometimes, like the vitalists, we abuse science because it ignores life. But there is only a short distance we can go on the teleological program" (Mead, 1927a: 171). The short distance is to make the point that life is more than mechanism alone; but Mead never went further to join the vitalists in positing vital forces or in claiming that life processes could not be studied scientifically. Mead was not siding with the vitalists versus the mechanists; he was merely stating that mechanism alone fails to explain the dynamics of life processes because it neglects the special properties of self-organizing, purposive, living systems.

Although the vitalists resisted the scientific analysis of living things—including human conduct—Mead did not. Taking a scientific approach, Mead stated: "There is no conflict between that teleological statement of [the world], on the one hand, and the mechanical, on the other. Science does not feel any conflict there" (Mead, 1936: 272). Science can study both mechanism and process; and in fact Mead argued that scientists should study both. "In biological science you bring in both these points of view" (Mead, 1936: 269). There is no need for conflict between the two types of study. For example, the biologist can study either mechanism or process. "If he reduces the reality of the life process to the means he is using, he becomes a mechanist. If the life process appears to him a reality that has emerged out of the physical world, and his study is of the conditions under which it maintains itself, he is a teleologist" (Mead, 1932: 35). As another example, Mead contrasted the work of the doctor and the district attorney in dealing with a murder (Mead, 1936: 269). The doctor who does the autopsy gives a mechanistic account of the means of the murder; the district attorney gives a teleological account that focuses on the "ends which the murderer had in view." Both accounts are completely legitimate, and there need be no conflict between them. They can be woven into one unified empirical explanation.

Only when advocates of pure mechanism or pure teleology deny the validity of the other approach are the positions in conflict.

> These two attitudes come into conflict with each other only if on the one hand he [the mechanist] denies reality to the process because he can reduce to energy the objects that enter into it, and therefore refuses to recognize that the process that he is investigating is a reality that has arisen..." [Mead, 1932: 35].

On the other hand, the study of design and purpose conflicts with mechanism only if it becomes a vitalist, antiscientific doctrine that denies mechanism (Mead, 1932: 35; 1936: 292-325).

According to Mead both mechanism and teleology are merely postulates (Mead, 1936: 264-291). They are not dogma. Each carries with it distinctive methods and strategies for scientific research, with their own strengths and weaknesses. Both can be used to illuminate important facets of the empirical world. "There is, then, no real conflict between a mechanical and a teleological account of the world or of the facts of life" (Mead, 1936: 271).

Mead himself often interwove mechanical explanations in his theories. For example, Mead explained that the internal conversation that we carry on in our heads is the "mechanism of thought"; and describing oneself objectively, as if looking at oneself from the role of others, is the "mechanism of introspection" (Mead, 1913/1964: 146). "The mechanism by means of which we do our thinking when we face problems is inevitably a social mechanism," that is, having an internal conversation with oneself (Mead, 1914: 52). Referring to the internal conversation, Mead stated, "This mechanism is what makes reasoning possible" (Mead, 1927a: 145-146). Planning ahead to make purposive decisions requires knowledge about the results of our various possible actions; and Mead explained that "mechanisms of communication provide a means of indicating what the resultants [of those actions] will be" (Mead, 1927a: 159). Dealing with the questions of social organization, Mead stated, "Self-consciousness is a mechanism for social organization..." (Mead, 1927a: 160). This is only a small sample of the references that Mead made to mechanisms of behavior and social events. The main point is that Mead's emphasis on process and criticism of *purely* mechanical theories did not lead him to a radical rejection of all mechanism. He argued that we need a balanced approach that recognizes both mechanism and process.

Mead's opposition to mind-body dualism allows us to see why he opposed the separation of mechanistic and process theories of behavior. Mechanistic methods are well-suited to the study of the body, nervous system, the internal conversation with oneself, and so forth. Process theories are well-suited to the study of mental processes for creating goals, purposes, and so forth. In order to avoid dualistic theories of mind and body, there must be no artificial separation of mechanistic and process theories (Mead, 1927a: 171ff). "The two accounts or descriptions must be brought together, but without sacrifice of intelligibility" (Mead, 1927a: 172). Much of Mead's work was devoted to demonstrating that we can account for all of human behavior—both physical and mental—via scientific methods (Mead, 1903; 1909; 1910c; 1912; 1913; 1917a; 1923; 1924-25; 1932; 1934). In so doing, science could—and should—focus on both mechanism and process. "The mechanical and teleological situations together constitute the situation of body and mind; this alone can give a full explanation of conduct" (Mead, 1927a: 171). Although Mead was not able to produce a perfect synthesis of these two, his goal was to work toward such a synthesis.

> The two are necessary in an adequate statement of behavior. The task of behavior-psychology is thus to present a statement of the two. [For the present] they may not be included in one category and for the present remain in two; but as we have suggested, there is no reason for holding that they cannot be included in one. This is the aim of our future investigations [Mead, 1927a: 175].

Not surprisingly, Dewey came to a similar conclusion: "Nature *has* a mechanism. . . . But only a philosophy which hypostatizes isolated results...concludes that nature *is* a mechanism and only a mechanism" (Dewey, 1929: 248). Although Mead and Dewey opposed purely mechanical approaches to science, they advocated a balanced integration of mechanism and process.

OBJECTIVE PSYCHOLOGY

A nondualist analysis of human conduct, that integrates both mental and physical activity, played a central role in Mead's unified theory. Mead's methods for studying behavior are closely tied to his rejection of dualism and the introspective psychologies favored by dualistic thinkers. In order to avoid dualism, Mead advocated an objective, scientific approach to human conduct, placing humans *in* nature rather than above nature.

At various points, Mead described his form of objective psychology as "behavioristic psychology" (Mead, 1924-25; 1927a; 1927b; 1934; 1936). In order to avoid confusion about the term "behaviorism," let us make it clear that Mead's conception of behaviorism must be understood in terms of his own historical time frame. The term "behaviorism" had just been created and there was no consensus about its precise meaning. Mead stated,

> The behavioristic approach to an understanding of self, the mind, and reflective intelligence is not a well worked out technique; it is more an attitude than a specific doctrine. It is an attempt to deal with the phenomena of psychology from an objective viewpoint, from observation of conduct and action. It grew out of comparative psychology, and it has the advantage of being objective. . . . The general approach of behaviorism is not based on any doctrine or theory; it aims only to avoid introspection [Mead, 1927a: 106].[15]

In modern terms, this position is known as *methodological behaviorism*, and it is based on a commitment to objective methods more than to any specific set of findings or theories.

Mead saw behaviorism as a natural extension of scientific methods for establishing the basic laws of behavior.[16] "We are interested in finding the most general laws of correlation we can find." "We are trying to state the experience of the individual and situations in just as common terms as we can, and it is this which gives the importance to what we call behavioristic psychology" (Mead, 1934: 39).

Mead described two general ways to approach behavioristic psychology (Mead, 1936: 390ff): "One is to consider the [behavioral] process itself in an external way, or, as the psychologists would say, in an objective fashion; just consider the act itself and forget about consciousness. Watson is the representative of that type of behaviorism" (Mead, 1936: 390). Mead also described Pavlov's work as an example of this first type of behaviorism: Pavlov focused on overt behavior and the nervous system, but disregarded consciousness. Turning to the second type of behaviorism, Mead stated, "The other approach is that of Professor Dewey..." (Mead, 1936: 392). Dewey's approach considers the whole act, including both external and internal components, both objective and subjective, as one organic unity (Dewey, 1896). Mead closely allied himself with this second approach (Mead, 1903; 1910a; 1922; 1924-25; 1927a; 1934). Mead's and Dewey's form of behaviorism is easily distinguished from Watson's and Pavlov's form by its commitment to establishing a scientific analysis of the origin and function of the mind as an organic component of the whole of human conduct.

Some sociologists have asserted that Mead was not a behaviorist, citing as evidence his criticisms of Watson. However, Mead was only critical of *Watson's version* of behaviorism, faulting it for systematically excluding mind and covert processes (Mead, 1934: 10f, 101f). In order to avoid the problems of introspective psychology and dualism, Watson totally excluded subjective experience from his research program, producing a rather narrow form of behaviorism. In contrast, Mead conceived of behaviorism in a "wider sense" (Mead, 1934: 2f), as including both objective and subjective events. "I want to point out . . . that even when we come to the discussion of such 'inner' experience, we can approach it from the point of view of the behaviorist, provided that we do not too narrowly conceive this point of view," as Watson did (Mead, 1934: 5). By taking a wider view of behaviorism, Mead stated that "it is possible to account for [mental events] or deal with them in behavioristic terms which are precisely similar to those which Watson employs in dealing with non-mental psychological phenomena" (Mead, 1934: 10).

Mead thought of mind in completely naturalistic terms, to be studied with scientific methods: " . . . if we then conceive it functionally, and as a natural rather than a transcendental phenomenon, it becomes possible to deal with it in behavioristic terms. In short, it is not possible to deny the existence of mind or consciousness or mental phenomena, nor is it desirable to do so . . ." (Mead, 1934: 10). "This approach is one of particular importance because it is able to deal with the field of communication in a way which neither Watson nor the introspectionist can do" (Mead, 1934: 6).

For Mead, "the act . . . is the fundamental datum in both social and individual psychology when behavioristically conceived, and it has both an inner and an outer phase, an internal and an external aspect" (Mead, 1934: 8).[17] Mead's method for approaching the internal and external components of the act was to work "from the outside to the inside" (Mead, 1934: 8). Mead wrote that his social behaviorism was "particularly concerned with the rise of such [inner] experience within the process as a whole. It simply works from the outside to the inside instead of from the inside to the outside, so to speak, in its endeavor to determine how such [inner] experience does arise within the process" (Mead, 1934: 7-8). The method of working "from the outside to the inside" consists of looking first at empirical data on biology, external- ly visible behavior and social interaction, then trying to determine how these external variables give rise to subjective experiences and subse- quent actions. "We do not approach the organism from within." "The actual process begins at the periphery and goes to the center" (Mead, 1927a: 156).

Thus, Mead typically began his analysis of inner experiences with a discussion of the biological potential for symbolic interaction and the socialization process by which the child learns to use symbols to com- municate with others (Mead, 1912; 1924-25; 1927a; 1934). Objective data on biology and socialization allow us to analyze the development of the inner conversation of mind in a nondualistic manner.

Mead's emphasis on working from the outside to the inside ties back to the first part of the chapter, in which we saw how Mead linked together the numerous processes of his model—starting with evolution of the stars, planets, and living beings, the development of human societies and languages, then the socialization of the individual. This parallels Mead's behavioristic process of working from outside to the inside, revealing the compatibility of behavioral methods and process methods. Also, the behavioristic methodology is much more sociolog- ical than individualistic and introspective psychologies that assume the primacy of the mind and undervalue the importance of social ex- perience for the development of verbal and mental processes.

* * *

This ends the introduction to Mead's pragmatic philosophy and his approach to creating a unified empirical worldview. The remaining chapters utilize Mead's methods to organize the details of his writings into a unified theory that covers the full range of his work.

Part II

Mead's Unified Theory

Part II presents the details of Mead's unified theory. Although it would be ideal to present the whole theory at once, so that the whole and its unity were more salient than any particular part, such an idealistic method is not possible. The constraints of language and logical explication force us to build up the model from its parts. It is hoped that the reader will appreciate these limitations and not misinterpret our focus on specific topics as indicating that any specific topic is more important than the whole or that the first topics to be presented are more important than the later topics.

Perhaps the easiest way to keep the whole of Mead's system in view at once is to refer again to Figure 1 (see Chapter 1). This figure provides an overview of the whole of Mead's theory and may help the reader see how *all* the components of Mead's model are important for understanding the whole. A biological individual (a) is born into social and physical environments (b, c, and d). From those environments (e, f, and g) the individual acquires an increasingly complex repertoire of covert and overt behavior (h). As the person gains increasing skill, the person has increasing influence (i, j, and k) on both micro and macro society (b and c) and on the broader environmental systems (d). As all the components of the system are interconnected in an organic whole, changes in any part of the system can influence other parts, creating dynamic changes in the whole system.

The following chapters deal with all the components of Mead's theory, starting with the most basic and building to higher levels of complexity. The chapters begin with biology, then add the topics of language, mind, self, and society. This order of development follows Mead's own logic in several ways. It is true to Mead's own intellectual development, beginning with his graduate work on physiological psychology in Germany, next turning to his interest in signals, communication, language, mind, and self, then focusing increasing attention on macro society (as Mead did in the later decades of his life). The order of topics follows Mead's methods (Chapter 4) of working from the outside to the inside (starting with biology, language, and society to explain the emergence of mind and self), then returning to explain how inside mental processes affect external things (such as social interaction and society). It also parallels evolutionary processes that start from simple biological beginnings and move to the emergence of language, mind, self, and society. Finally, it follows the development of the child from earliest infancy as the child becomes an increasingly verbal and social being.

5

The Biological Individual

For Mead, knowledge about the biological individual was important for creating a unified theory. In Figure 1 (see Chapter 1), all the arrows of influence operate through the biological individual. The actions of the biological individual influence and modify both the physical and social environments (the upward arrows in Figure 1); and the physical and social environments influence the biological individual (the downward arrows). "This determining relationship is bilateral. The environment determines the organism as fully as the organism determines the environment" (Mead, 1938: 412). "Since the organism and environment determine each other and are mutually dependent for their existence, it follows that the life-process, to be adequately understood, must be considered in terms of their interrelations" (Mead, 1934: 130).

From early in his career, Mead was interested in using biological theories—especially concerning *evolution* and *animal behavior*—to understand the life process. In Mead's time, evolutionary theory was revolutionizing Western thought about the place of humans in nature, placing us closer to the apes than was ever before suspected (Mead, 1923/1964: 265). The evolutionary approach to animal and human behavior lay behind the development of Mead's behavioral theory of the act (Mead, 1924-25). Mead's graduate school training and research in physiology in Germany gave him a life-long interest in the physiological bases of behavior. In a related vein, Mead studied the biologically inherited components of animal behavior in order to explain the roots of human behavior. Throughout his work, Mead integrated evolution, physiology, and theories of animal behavior with the other elements of his unified theory in order to create a unified, nondualistic model.

EVOLUTION

As we saw in prior chapters, evolutionary theory played a central role in the development of pragmatism and in Mead's rejection of dualism. Evolutionary theory placed humans—mind and body together—in nature, to be studied scientifically. In Mead's non-dualistic theory, there is no split between biological and mental or social processes. Although Mead distinguished between the "biologic individual" and the "socially self-conscious individual," he pointed out that "they are not on separate planes, but play back and forth into each other, and constitute, under most conditions, an experience which appears to be cut by no lines of cleavage" (Mead, 1934: 347). Physiological, mental, and social processes are all part of the life process. There is a continuous, dynamic interaction between biology, society, and the self-conscious individual (as indicated by the cycles of arrows in Figure 1).

Mead began with the assumption that humans are a product of the evolutionary process, as are all other living things. Therefore, the key to understanding human nature lay in the scientific study of our place in the evolutionary process.

Mead used evolutionary theories to synthesize a broad range of data into a coherent overview of the entire panorama of life—from the origins of life on earth and the evolution of new species to the emergence of the human capacity for language, mind, and self-conscious behavior. Although recent evolution is of most direct relevance to understanding human nature, the entire sweep of evolution fit into Mead's unified theory. For example, theories of the evolution of the stars and planets were more attractive to him than was the static Newtonian model of the universe: "Compare for instance the excitement of Eddington's or Jeans' histories of stellar bodies with the monotony of a Newtonian mechanical structure..." (Mead, 1932: 46).[18] Although evolutionary theories of the universe and life on earth led Mead to acknowledge the insignificantly small role of human life in the whole cosmos, he concluded that the scientific perspective makes humans more "at home" in nature than had prior dualistic worldviews that separated mind from body and focused more attention on mind than on the body and its physical environment (Mead, 1923).

Evolutionary theory clearly views humans as animals that are interacting with a physical environment. "The scientific attitude contemplates our physical habitat as primarily the environment of man who is the first cousin once removed of the arboreal anthropoid ape..." (Mead, 1923/1964: 265). Even though that environment is "transformed first through unreflective intelligence and then by reflective intelligence into the environment of a human society..." (Mead, 1923/1964: 265), the mental and social transformations do not ever lift humans out of nature to a transcendental realm: "Mind can never transcend the environment within which it operates" (Mead, 1932: 118). The same holds true, of course, for society: "Not only is man as an animal and as an inquirer into nature at home in the world, but the society of men is equally a part of the order of the universe" (Mead, 1923/1964: 264).

Mead frequently presented examples of animal behavior at various phylogenetic levels: unicellular organisms, ants, bees, termites, chicks, parrots, cats, dogs, oxen, monkeys, and so forth (Mead, 1907; 1924-25; 1927a; 1932; 1934; 1936). Most of the examples of animal behavior were used to illustrate the evolutionary steps leading up to human behavior. Mead conceived of consciousness as existing in varying degrees, ranging from simple feelings in lower species to reflective awareness in humans (Mead, 1932: 68f; 1924-25/1964: 278ff). He used animal examples to explain the biological and social prerequisites for the emergence of each higher form of consciousness that evolved. In so doing, Mead emphasized the continuity of humans with other life forms rather than trying to argue that humans were so different that animal data were irrelevant. It "is from a social nature of [the] kind exhibited in the conduct of lower forms that our human nature is evolved" (Mead, 1917-18/1964: 213). Although symbolic self-awareness "is perhaps the most critical in the development of man, it is after all only an elaboration of the social conduct of lower forms" (Mead, 1917-18/1964: 214). "I have wished to present mind as an evolution in nature..." (Mead, 1932: 85). We are thinking organisms who have evolved from more primitive forms, and only now are we gaining a scientific understanding of our place in nature. "It is a splendid adventure if we can rise to it" (Mead, 1923/1964: 266).

The comparative approach to animal behavior was the foundation for Mead's methodological behaviorism.

> There is an aspect of this [behavioristic] psychology that calls for an emphasis which I think has not been sufficiently given it. It is not simply the objectivity of this psychology which has commended it. . . . But behavioristic psychology, coming in by the door of the study of animals lower than man, has perforce shifted its interest from psychical states to external conduct [Mead, 1924-25/1964: 267].

Comparing the overt behavior of animals at various phylogenetic levels allowed Mead to trace the evolution of increasingly complex forms of responses and identify the biological and social precursors of each step of increasingly complex behavior, including the emergence of the capacity for reflective intelligence and self-awareness in humans. Using this method, Mead was able to explain the emergence of subjective processes (Mead, 1924-25; 1934), whereas dualistic and introspective psychologies had merely taken these as given and failed to analyze their origins.

Given his evolutionary perspective, it is only natural that Mead often tried—given the limited data available at his time—to trace the behavioral evolution of early humans. Among his points were these. Early languages evolved from grunts and groans that were made from sudden changes of breathing (Mead, 1912/1964: 136). The "primitive mood of all language . . . starts with groans or grunts accompanied by a directive symbol. At first the sound is not even functional; it is merely a disturbance of rhythmical breathing called forth by a change in the social situation" (Mead, 1927a: 160). Mead often compared children with primitive people, noting, for example, that awarenesses of others "arise earlier than the self, both in the child and the race" (Mead, 1914: 63). Primitive peoples often viewed the world much as children do, for example, attributing social qualities to physical objects (Mead, 1914: 31; 1927a: 141, 146, 157, 187). Compared with moderns, members of small, primitive societies could more easily "enter into sympathetic relationship with every member of the group," which makes social organization quite different from that in large-scale modern societies (Mead, 1914: 82, 104f; see also Chapter 10). He used observations on the socialization of children in primitive societies to highlight problems with modern educational practices and suggested methods more in tune with our human biological nature (Mead, 1910b).

Mead used modified versions of the theory of natural selection when developing his own theories about mental and social events that appeared to be based on selective processes (Mead, 1908; 1924-25; 1934: 16, 134, 214f, 250f; 1936: 164ff, 367, 371, 381). He correctly described natural selection as a "trial-and-error" process in which "slight variations" and "mutations" led to the emergence of new forms over "thousands of years" (Mead, 1936: 364f). His theories of reflective intelligence and scientific research were based on selective processes that were consciously designed to attain the most successful results without the inefficiencies of trial-and-error processes (Mead, 1934: 90-100; 1936: 371). "Human intelligence . . . deliberately selects one from among the several alternative responses . . . to make possible the most adequate and harmonious solution. . ." (Mead, 1934: 98). Mead also described social change and evolution in terms of selective processes (Mead, 1936: 365ff, 383f).

Mead's evolutionary perspective did not portray animals—including humans—in passive roles, as if solely the products of evolutionary forces or genetic determinism. According to some earlier statements of evolutionary theory, "the individual is really passive as over against the influences which are affecting it all the time. But what needs now to be recognized is that the character of the organism is a determinant of its environment" (Mead, 1934: 215). A species selects the subset of its environment to which it will respond; and its actions alter that environment, thereby modifying its own habitat. "The organism in a real sense is determinative of its environment" (Mead, 1934: 215). Thus, evolution has produced active organisms that select, change, and modify their worlds. "All species in some sense control their environments" (Mead, 1938: 489). "Here we have the organism as acting and determining its environment" (Mead, 1934: 25). This is, of course, true of humans and human societies: "But it has been left to man to attain the largest control over the environment..." (Mead, 1938: 489). "The whole onward struggle of mankind on the face of the earth is such a determination of the life that shall exist about it and such a control of physical objects as determine and affect its own life. The community as such creates its environment by being sensitive to it" (Mead, 1934: 250).

For Mead, evolutionary theory revolutionized philosophy by revealing that our ideas about mind and philosophy—like all ideas—are products of biological and social evolution.

> The evolutionary point of view has had more than one important result for philosophical thought. ... Not only can we trace in the history of thought the evolution of the conception of evolution, but we find ourselves with a consciousness which we conceive of as evolved; the contents and the forms of these contents can be looked upon as the products of development [Mead, 1908/1964: 82].

Therefore, even philosophy and the history of ideas must be explained in terms of scientific, evolutionary models: "All the distinctions must be explained by the same general laws as those which are appealed to to account for animal organs and functions" (Mead, 1908/1964: 82). Again we see Mead's commitment to unifying all facets of his theory —biology, psychology, sociology, and even the history of ideas—in terms of one internally consistent set of general laws.

BEHAVIOR

Mead approached the study of psychology by studying animal and human behavior (Mead, 1924-25/1964: 267ff). Several facets of his psychology deserve attention.

The Act. Mead (1903; 1910a) was significantly influenced by Dewey's (1896) criticism of theories that attempted to explain complex behavior in terms of simple stimulus-response (S-R) reflexes, in which a stimulus elicits a response in a simple mechanical manner. In order to deal with complex acts, Mead used information about animal and human behavior to develop a psychological theory that incorporated multiple factors that were integrated in an organic, "dynamic whole ... no part of which can be considered or understood by itself..." (Mead, 1934: 7; see also Mead, 1934: 111f).

The act was central to Mead's psychological theories. "The act, then, and not the tract, is the fundamental datum in both social and individual psychology when behavioristically conceived..." (Mead, 1934: 8). Judging from the context, "the tract" refers to tracts in the central nervous system. Even though Mead did discuss neural tracts in detail, the study of the act was more important because it focused on a larger organic process, whereas the central nervous system provided only a part of the mechanism for that process.

> What the behaviorist does, or ought to do, is take the complete act, the whole process of conduct as the unit of his account. In doing that he has to take into account not simply the nervous system but also the rest of the organism, for the nervous system is only a specialized part of the entire organism [Mead, 1934: 111].

Mead described the act as an organic unity consisting of four major components, none of which is independent of the others (Mead, 1914: 27-31; 1938: 3-25). Each part is interrelated with the others to produce a unified, organic whole. Although "analysis breaks up, for the time being, this organic unity and these relationships" (Mead, 1914: 31), Dewey (1896) and Mead (1903; 1938) stressed the "wholeness" and "unity" of all parts of the act. "In this respect they are not composite parts of the act, though the different stages are parts of the whole as a process" (Mead, 1938: 452).

The four main parts of the act are the (1) impulse, (2) perception, (3) manipulation, and (4) consummation (Mead, 1938). These four are seen in many organisms, such as dogs, apes, and humans (Mead, 1938: 7, 24, 136). When a dog is hungry, hunger is the *impulse* to look for something to eat. Looking is a form of selective *perception,* as the dog selectively scans the environment for things to eat. If food is found, the dog *manipulates* it—perhaps pulling it apart with its mouth and paws—and then the dog *consumes* it. The manipulative phase is the means to the ends of consummation.

Although the four parts of the act sometimes *appear* to be linked in a linear order, they actually interpenetrate to form one organic process: Facets of each part are present at all times from the beginning of the act to the end, such that each part affects the others. For example, at the beginning of the act, images of later parts arise and influence the subsequent course of the act. When we first notice that we are hungry, we may have images and thoughts of all parts of the act— looking through the refrigerator, making a sandwich and enjoying eating it—and these cognitions influence how we proceed with the act. "Our conduct is made up of a series of steps which follow each other, and the later steps may be already started and influence the earlier ones. The thing we are going to do is playing back on what we are doing now" (Mead, 1934: 71).

Let us examine all four parts in greater detail. First, the impulse is the precondition for the remainder of the act, the way that hunger is the precondition for seeking food and eating. When we are hungry, "the stomach hurts, and the things we manipulate are interesting, and the food is agreeable" (Mead, 1938: 452). Hunger sensitizes the organism for *all* parts of the act of finding and consuming food (Mead, 1914: 28). "We start with the impulse that sensitizes the organism..." to relevant stimuli, manipulations, and the final results of the act (Mead, 1927a: 121f). Thus, later parts of the act, such as "the result of the act may be [influential] in the beginning of the process..." (Mead, 1927a: 122).

The impulse to act arouses images of all phases of the act. The impulse of hunger brings up *sense imagery* of various types of food, along with *motor imagery* of manipulating and consuming the food (Mead, 1914: 27-31). Thus, in the form of images, the later phases of the act are present and influencing each step of the act from the very beginning. These images give us an awareness of the whole act, both at the beginning and as we proceed through it. The sense imagery guides selective perception, as we look for relevant stimuli (Mead, 1914: 28). The motor imagery consists of a "readiness to respond" that influences the type of manipulation that will be done later (Mead, 1927a: 129). As the individual progresses through the act, environmental conditions and stimuli constantly change, which leads to changes in imagery and continual "mid-course" adjustments in the direction of the act. Because all four components are interlocked in an organic whole, each influences the others through all possible feedback and feedforward loops, allowing the individual to make continuous adjustments to current conditions at each moment during the act. Thus, the act is constructed as a dynamic series of adjustments in which ever-changing conditions lead to continuous alterations in the current nature of impulses, sensory imagery, motor imagery, and responses. This is clearly different from the S-R model of behavior, in which a stimulus merely elicits a response in a mechanical manner.

The second phase of the act, perception, consists of an active and selective search for stimuli. "The process of sensing is itself an activity" (Mead, 1938: 3). For example, the eyes are active in looking for things, focusing, adjusting to different light conditions. Attention is selective (Mead, 1900/1964: 14-18, 20; 1910b/1964: 120f; 1914: 28, 64f; 1924-25/1964: 272, 275ff; 1932: 5; 1934: 25, 65, 95, 132, 215, 245, 337f, 341; 1938: 5), as we search for stimuli relevant to the current impulse, possible future manipulations and the anticipated results of the act. "The mechanism of this selection is frequently found in the anticipatory presentation of the object which is of importance" (Mead, 1938: 5), for example the types of food that are imagined.

Perception involves two components: incoming stimuli and the mental images they call up. The "precept is a construct in which the sensuous stimulation is merged with imagery which comes from past experience" (Mead, 1912/1964: 134; see also 1912/1964: 134-138; 1938: 3). As individuals gain experience with all four parts of various acts, the stimuli perceived at any point call up images of all parts of the act. "A perception has in it, therefore, all the elements of an act ... represented by the imagery arising out of past reactions" (Mead, 1938: 3). Thus, "a perception is ... a collapsed act." "This imagery gives us the result of the act before we carry it out" (Mead, 1914: 29).

For the most part, images of all parts of the act are based on past experience with those parts (Mead, 1912; 1934: 338; 1938: 3, 54, 161, 227). However, in some cases, imagery may be based on innate mechanisms rather than past experience. In humans and other mammals, newborn babies perceive and respond correctly to the nipple without any prior experience. "This does not necessarily imply past experience. In the case of young infants and certain lower animal forms ... actions which perception invites may lead to successful conclusions which cannot have been experienced" before (Mead, 1938: 12).

Although most images are based on memories of the past (Mead, 1912/1964: 134), images "are essentially forward-looking" (Mead, 1903/1964: 57; see also Mead, 1934: 344). The perception of immediate stimuli allows the individual to sense possible future directions of the whole act, based on past experience. Perceptions involve images of the *means* and *ends* that lie ahead in parts three and four of the act. "The perceptual world is made up of ends and means" (Mead, 1914: 31) that help guide the act to consummation.

Mead's theory of perception is quite different from that of S-R theories, in which a stimulus elicits a response, the way a tap on the knee elicits a knee-jerk response. For Mead, the stimulus only sets the occasion for images and responses; it does not cause the response, as in the S-R model (Mead, 1903/1964: 37; 1927a: 112). It sets the occasion for many possible images, which allow various means and ends of the act to be evaluated, in search of "the most adequate and harmonious solution..." (Mead, 1934: 98).

Perception gives us awareness of objects at a distance. Vision is the most important distance sense modality, though hearing and smelling are important, too (Mead, 1938: 23). Mead described the properties of objects that are perceived at a distance—such as their color, sound and odor—as "secondary properties" (Mead, 1907; 1927a: 107f, 117ff, 125; 1932: 123ff, 133ff; 1938: 17ff, 73f, 295ff). Only after making contact with an object can we sense the object's "primary properties" such as its weight, solidity, and resistance to movement.

The third part of the act is manipulation. After perceiving a hammer at a distance and approaching it, we pick it up and hit a nail. Even before we get to the manipulation phase, the attitude of manipulation response is already present.

> We are ready to grasp the hammer before we reach it, and the attitude of manipulatory response directs the approach. What we are going to do determines the line of approach and in some sense its manner. It is the later process already aroused in the central nervous system, controlling the earlier, which constitutes the teleological [or purposive] character of the act [Mead, 1938: 24].

Again we see how the parts of the act blend into and affect each other.

Manipulation involves physical contact with objects (Mead, 1938: 23), and this gives us an awareness of their primary properties (weight, solidity, resistance). Contact experience with the primary properties of a stimulus helps give meaning to the secondary properties that are perceived at a distance, before contact is made. When a child first sees and picks up a hammer, the feelings of weight and hardness help the child understand the primary properties of the hammer, and this gives meaning to the secondary (visual) properties of a hammer the next time the child sees one at a distance. The sight of the object has assimilated to it "imagery of contact sensation" (Mead, 1910c/1964: 126). As individuals have repeated contact experiences, they gain a better understanding of things perceived at a distance, because they know what those things will be like when they contact and manipulate them.

Contact and manipulation in animals are often simple, providing limited information about the primary properties of stimuli. However, humans have the capacity to manipulate things more subtly, especially by using the hands; and the extra contact experience helps us gain much greater understanding of the primary properties of the stimuli. Mead frequently emphasized the importance of the hand in gaining contact information (Mead, 1907/1964: 78-80; 1917b: 184; 1927a: 119, 121; 1932: 60, 107, 131, 134; 1934: 184f, 248f, 362f; 1938: 24). "In manipulation or contact the hand is of fundamental importance, and its high development is a mark of the intelligence of the human" (Mead, 1927a: 119).

Manipulation is "instrumental" in accomplishing things (Mead, 1938: 24). Namely, it provides the means to reach the ends of consummation.

The last phase of the act is consummation (Mead, 1938: 23ff, 445-457). "The common illustration is that of eating" (Mead, 1938: 136). When food is consumed, hunger gradually subsides and the act of eating eventually comes to an end. Consummation completes the act by "satisfying the impulse," the way that eating satisfies hunger. "Consummation is satisfaction and, if you like, happiness..." (Mead, 1938: 136).

Consummation defines the value of the act (Mead, 1938: 445-453). "Within the field of consummation all the adjectives of value obtain immediately. There objects...are good, bad, and indifferent, beautiful or ugly, and lovable or noxious" (Mead, 1938: 25). "In terms of these values we can analyze the act" (Mead, 1938: 452). Consummation also provides a key to understanding aesthetic values (Mead, 1938: 454-459). Whereas perception reveals an object's secondary properties (e.g., odor, sight) and manipulation reveals its primary properties (e.g., weight, solidity), consummation reveals its ultimate use, value and reality. "The reality of the object is found in the consummation..." (Mead, 1927a: 124). The realities of consummation give value and meaning to our understanding of the secondary properties of stimuli we perceive at a distance and the primary properties of stimuli we contact during manipulation.

Sometimes perceiving stimuli at a distance produces illusions (Mead, 1927a: 125, 162f; 1932: 37, 132); but we may not know that they are illusions until we attempt to manipulate or consume the object indicated by the stimuli. When a child sees a shimmering mirage over a desert, the child may think that it is water. The test of the reality of the perception is to approach the stimuli and try to manipulate (Mead, 1927a: 123) or consume (Mead, 1927a: 124) the perceived water. Although a perception about the world may *seem* true, it takes on reality only if it helps bring some functional act to completion. "If it cannot fit into the organization of such an act we dismiss it as illusory: e.g., the apparent wetness of the shimmer above the desert sand cannot be fitted into the act of going to and drinking the illusory water" (Mead, 1932: 132). "In the immediate perceptual world what we can handle is the reality to which what is seen and heard must be brought to the test, if we are to escape illusion and hallucination" (Mead, 1932: 37). "[R]eality reduces to contact-experience." "Contact is what gives reality to the stimulus" (Mead, 1927a: 120).

Mead stated that when the four phases of the act can take place without any delays or problems, the act is rather automatic (Mead, 1903; 1910c). Impulse leads to selective perception, manipulation of appropriate objects and consummation. This sequence is an organic whole that is fairly well established by our biological nature or well-learned habits.

The four phases of the act become more complex when the act is blocked by problems or obstacles (Mead, 1903; 1910c; 1914: 28ff; 1934: 98ff; 1938: 6ff, 82). "The situation out of which the difficulty, the problem, springs is a lack of adjustment between the individual and his world" (Mead, 1938: 6). Such blocks inhibit the continuation of the act as it would naturally occur, and lead to the search for alternative routes of action. Lower organisms (and young children) typically do this search in a trial-and-error manner; but human adults are likely to use more reflective and intelligent methods (Mead, 1938: 7). The emergence and use of reflective intelligence are discussed in detail in Chapter 6.

Physiology. Mead's graduate work in physiological psychology in Germany had a significant impact on his later theories. In many parts of his writings and lectures, he presented information on the central nervous system and other physiological systems to provide a partial explanation of the mechanisms of perception, thought, emotions, and action (Mead, 1895; 1903; 1909; 1922; 1924-25; 1927a; 1932; 1934; 1936).[19]

Two main themes appear in Mead's writings on physiology. First, Mead advocated using physiological data when possible to explain the biological mechanisms of behavior. Second, he was critical of scientists who claimed that physiological mechanisms *alone* could explain mental processes that involve language and symbolic thought: Clearly cognitive processes cannot develop until an individual learns language and inner speech through symbolic social interaction. These two positions are not contradictory. For Mead, the central nervous system was a necessary but not sufficient condition for symbolic thought. His criticisms were directed at physiologists who claimed that the central nervous system was not only necessary but sufficient for explaining thought, and who therefore neglected the role of social, symbolic experience.

First, Mead was quite aware of the importance of physiological psychology for providing data on the biological mechanisms of thought and behavior; and in numerous places in his work he used physiological data to make biology an integral component of his unified theory, without any dualistic separation of mind and body. He explained the evolution of increasingly complex physiological mechanisms of behavior that freed vertebrates from the rigid stimulus-response patterns seen in the most primitive species (Mead, 1924-25/1964: 278ff). Advanced neural mechanisms evolved because they gave animals an "immense advantage" in responding in a flexible manner to avoid dangerous contacts or obtain satisfying ones (Mead, 1932: 136). Mead attempted to specify the biological mechanisms needed for flexible behavior (Mead, 1924-25; 1932; 1934). "We have learned in recent years that it is the function of the central nervous system in the higher forms to connect every response potentially with every other response in the organism. In a sense all responses are so interconnected by way of interrelated innervation and inhibition" (Mead, 1932: 124-125).[20] This high level of neural interconnectedness represents a significant advance over the simple stimulus-response mechanisms prevalent in lower species; it allows all elements of a species' behavioral repertoire to be joined together in almost any combination. "The mechanism by which this is accomplished is the cerebrum." "The cerebrum ... is an organ which integrates the vast variety of responses, including the lower reflexes..." (Mead, 1932: 126).

Mead was especially interested in the mechanisms by which advanced animals made choices among the variety of responses they could perform in any situation. "We know that conscious processes are dependent upon a high development of an encephalon which is the outgrowth of the nervous mechanism of distance stimulation and of the delayed responses which distant stimuli make possible" (Mead, 1932: 66). Choice depends on the ability to delay immediate reactions, respond to the future consequences of different alternative actions, and select the better ones: "The whole of such [an advanced] nervous system provides ... the mechanism for selection with reference to distant futures, and this selection endows surrounding objects with the values and meanings which this future subtends" (Mead, 1932: 66).[21]

When dealing with human choice and purposive action, Mead said: "Human intelligence, by means of the physiological mechanisms of the human central nervous system, deliberately selects one from among the several alternative responses which are possible in the given problematic environmental situation..." (Mead, 1934: 98). From this,

Mead concluded "that the purposive element in behavior has a physiological seat..." (Mead, 1934: 100).[22] A few pages later, he stated:

> I have attempted to point out that the meanings of things, our ideas of them, answer to the structure of the organism in its conduct with reference to things. The structure which makes this possible was found primarily in the central nervous system.... The central nervous system, in short, enables the individual to exercise conscious control over his behavior [Mead, 1934: 117].

Naturally, Mead was aware of the limitations of physiological data. The central nervous system is so complex that even today physiological data can explain only a small portion of the biological mechanisms that mediate delayed response, choice, and purposive action. After tracing the emergence of mind and self in vertebrate evolution, Mead concluded: "The structure of the central nervous system is too minute to enable us to show the corresponding structural changes in the paths of the brain. It is only in the behavior of the human animal that we can trace this evolution" (Mead, 1924-25/1964: 283). Mead reached similar conclusions elsewhere (Mead, 1934: 24, 26, 39). His approach to mind and higher mental processes through the study of behavior will be presented in Chapters 6 through 8.

This brings us to the second theme in Mead's writings about physiological mechanisms: his criticisms of physiologists who claimed that mental processes could be fully explained in terms of the central nervous system. Mead argued that even if *all* the data were available on the central nervous system, those data *alone* would not provide a full explanation of mind, consciousness, self, and complex human action.

In *Mind, Self, and Society,* Mead developed the argument that we can find a partial explanation for mental events in terms of the central nervous system (Mead, 1934: 70f, 83ff, 96ff). However, a few pages later (Mead, 1934: 106-107), he asked whether groups of responses in the nervous system are all that are needed to explain consciousness. "We can find part of the necessary mechanism of such conduct in the central nervous system." "The question now is whether the mere excitement of the set of these groups of responses is what we mean by an idea." In the following pages Mead answered the question in the negative. Only through social processes—through symbolic social interaction with others—does a person learn language and learn to carry on the inner conversation that we identify as mind. "The process of getting an idea is ... a process of intercourse ... a social process" (Mead, 1934: 107). Therefore we need to study social behavior and interaction—the whole of an individual's acts—to explain mental experience.[23] "Instead of assuming that the experienced world as such is inside of a head, located at that point at which certain nervous disturbances are going on, what the behaviorist does is to relate the world of experience to the whole act of the organism" (Mead, 1934: 111). This clearly reflects Mead's unifying approach: It does not deny the importance of neural mechanisms; but it locates them within a larger perspective on human activity and life processes.

The central nervous system *alone* is merely a mechanism. "And this mechanism is only a series of paths" (Mead, 1903/1964: 56; see also Mead, 1934: 21-22). The neural pathways of the human brain give us the potential for language, internal conversation, and reflective intelligence; but only through social experience does the individual develop that potential and acquire symbolic mental faculties. Thus, mind consists of more than nerve pathways: Mental processes emerge only when the individual engages in symbolic interaction with others, within the larger group. "The process does appear in a certain sense in the central nervous system, as we take the role of others; still, the unity or pattern does not belong to the organism but to the group" (Mead, 1927a: 173). Therefore, the study of mind requires attention to more than brain structure: "The logical function of physiological psychology is to give a statement of the world of the physical sciences. . . . In my judgment, however, we must recognize not only a corporeal individual, but a social and even logical individual. . ." (Mead, 1903/1964: 57).

At numerous places in his writings and lectures, Mead was critical of those physiological psychologists who claimed that the central nervous system *alone* would explain consciousness, as this view neglected the social side of mental processes (Mead, 1900; 1903; 1924-25; 1927a; 1934). Even today, many physiologists overemphasize the role of neurotransmitters and neural structures as the causes of thinking—disregarding the importance of social and symbolic variables.

Because biologists and physiologists usually do not analyze mind in terms of social processes, they often describe mind as merely a subjective experience that parallels brain activity. This approach, called "parallelism," was unacceptable to Mead if it neglected the social and symbolic processes needed to explain the nature and origin[24] of the inner flow of verbal thoughts. In addition, parallelism can lead to dualistic theories, as it retains the mind-body distinctions from traditional philosophy. "The term [parallelism] is unfortunate in that it carries with it the distinction between mind and body, between the psychical and the physical" (Mead, 1934: 38). "We do not want two languages, one of certain physical facts and one of certain conscious facts'' (Mead, 1934: 40). Mind and body must be treated together as parts of the same process in order to avoid creating dualistic theories (Mead, 1927a: 171-175; 1930b).[25]

Physiologists are especially likely to do an injustice to the subjective side of mental activity when they describe mind as an ''epiphenomenon''—a mere side effect of neural activity. As this approach suggests that mind is of trivial importance compared with the brain, it allows physiologists to neglect social-symbolic variables and focus all their attention on the central nervous system. Mead rejected this position because it bifurcates the world (creating a dualism between the brain and the epiphenomenal mind), and it portrays mental events as ''harmless conscious shadows'' of neural activity that require no special study (Mead, 1924-25/1964: 269).

Although Mead argued that physiology *alone* cannot provide an adequate theory of mind and behavior, he did not denounce physiological research on neural mechanisms. ''Nor does this mean that the physiologist should abandon his effort to get back to chemical reactions...'' (Mead, 1927a: 175). Mead stated that when physiological and social psychology were used in conjunction, each would complement the other; and *together* they would constitute a unified theory (Mead, 1909; 1927a: 175). ''The two are necessary in an adequate statement of behavior'' (Mead, 1927a: 175). A complete explanation of mind requires attention to *both* physiology and social psychology.

> It is evident that we must be as much beholden to social science to present and analyze the social group ... as we are beholden to physiological science to present and analyze the physical complex which is the precondition of our physical consciousness. In other words, a social psychology should be the counterpart of physiological psychology [Mead, 1909/1964: 103].

If this balanced synthesis of physiology and social psychology were accepted, Mead was willing to advocate strict parallelism: ''From a logical point of view a social psychology is strictly parallel to a physiological psychology'' (Mead, 1909/1964: 104). In a nondualistic model, the two must fit together perfectly, with no lines of cleavage (Mead, 1927a: 175; 1932: 52f, 65f, 76, 80).[26] Thus, Mead was willing to espouse parallelism if both physiological psychology and social psychology were integrated in a nondualistic model, with a balanced emphasis given to each.

Instincts. From the study of the behavior of animals and young children, it is clear that some types of behavior must be explained primarily in terms of biological causes. At the turn of the century, many psychologists attempted to explain the biologically programmed components of behavior in terms of instincts. Over the decades, instinct theories have been replaced by theories of reflexes, innate behavior, and fixed action patterns; nevertheless, modern psychology still recognizes that certain elements of animal and human behavior are biologically programmed. Although instinct theories are no longer generally accepted, we can appreciate why Mead—given the scientific information available to him—turned to instinct theories as a means of dealing with the biological components of behavior and trying to understand their influences on human behavior and society.

Mead frequently incorporated instincts in his theories of animal and human behavior. In lower animals, behavior sometimes is directly based on instincts. In humans, instincts lie behind the impulses, which are the first part—the precondition—of the act. Mead was aware of the problems in attempting to identify instincts (Mead, 1914: 32ff, 41), and he never committed himself to a definitive list of instincts that he presumed to be operating. In a couple of places, he cited McDougall's list of eleven instincts[27] and stated that "these would probably be the instincts most widely accepted by those who are willing to accept human instincts at all" (Mead, 1909/1964: 97; see also Mead, 1914: 41). The social instincts—such as hostility, reproduction, parental care—played the most important part in Mead's theories, as these appeared to explain the underlying causes for human social interaction. Mead stated, "Whatever the list of instincts may be, there are certain social tendencies..." (Mead, 1914: 33).

Mead recognized that instincts operate differently at different phylogenetic levels (Mead, 1924-25/1964: 278ff). The behavior of insects is more highly determined than is the behavior of the vertebrates. The behavior of advanced species is often quite modifiable, with human behavior being the most malleable. Nevertheless, even the behavior of lower species is not rigidly determined.

> The instincts even in the lower animal forms have lost their rigidity. They are found to be subject to modification by experience, and the nature of the animal is found to be not a bundle of instincts but an organization within which these congenital habits function to bring about complex acts—acts which are in many cases the result of instincts which have modified each other. Thus new activities arise which are not the simple expression of bare instincts [Mead, 1917-18/1964: 212].

When turning to humans, Mead expected the instincts to be much more malleable than in the lower species. For example, the instinctual response of attacking an enemy may be modified to consist of merely asserting oneself against others (Mead, 1917-18/1964: 214). Parental instincts may lead to caring for others in general, emerging at different times as kindliness, charity, or philanthropy (Mead, 1930).

Mead's balanced view of biological and social determinants of behavior allowed him to avoid taking an extreme position in the nature and nurture controversy. "The quarrel over instincts is unnecessary." "The distinction between instinct and habit comes down to degrees of modification" (Mead, 1927a: 113). Behavior can be placed anywhere on a continuum from highly modifiable to highly unmodifiable, and the location of any given behavior on the continuum is an empirical question. Although Mead expected human behavior to be more malleable than the behavior of lower species, his model included both nature and nurture at all phylogenetic levels, including human beings. "The way in which we move our legs is inherited, but it is subject to great change. You can teach a horse different gaits, but the movements involved are fundamentally instinctive" (Mead, 1927a: 114). The behavior of both species reflects a mixture of nature and nurture, though there is more modifiability in humans.

Mead did not believe that human conduct reflected the direct, unmediated expression of instincts. He discriminated carefully between instincts and impulses: The bases of human conduct

> are best termed "impulses," and not "instincts," because they are subject to extensive modifications in the life-history of individuals, and these modifications are so much more extensive than those to which the instincts of lower animal forms are subject that the use of the term "instinct" in describing the behavior of normal adult human individuals is seriously inexact [Mead, 1934: 337].

Thus, for Mead, human conduct springs from impulses that reflect modified versions of instincts: "Self-conscious conduct arises out of controlled and organized impulse, and impulses arise out of social instincts ... " (Mead, 1909/1964: 98). "Human nature still remains an organization of instincts which have mutually affected each other" (Mead, 1917-18/1964: 214). Therefore the roots of human behavior can be understood, in part, by the study of animal instincts. For example, when dealing with the impulse to help others, Mead said: "It is an impulse which we can trace back to animals lower than man" (Mead, 1930/1964: 392).

As children gain the capacity to reflect consciously on their own actions, they can further modify the instincts, lifting them above the mechanical level. Self-consciousness "lifts these instincts out of the level of the mechanical response to biologically determined stimuli and brings them within the sweep of self-conscious direction inside the larger group activity" (Mead, 1917-18/1964: 215).

As Mead viewed impulses as complex products of instincts that can interact with each other, be modified by experience, and be consciously controlled, he expected impulses to be hard to analyze: "It is, of course, difficult if not impossible to isolate the fundamental impulses of our natures" (Mead, 1930/1964: 394). Nevertheless, in one place, Mead presented a "roughly fashioned catalogue of primitive human impulses" (Mead, 1934: 348f), and it has certain parallels with McDougall's list of instincts.

Mead identified two components in the instinctive act: internal emotional responses and externally visible gestures. Because he conceived of impulses as being based on instincts, impulses could also involve emotional elements and externally visible signal qualities. First, according to the physiological psychologists, the stimuli that elicit instinctive acts activate "vaso-motor processes" (Mead, 1895: 164) that produce the "visceral disturbances" that are experienced as the basic emotional "feelings" (Mead, 1903: 95). In a later formulation of the physiology of emotions, Mead traced emotional feelings to the "innervation of sensory nerves," which triggered "tracts which went down to the viscera, and these certainly were aligned with the emotional experiences" (Mead, 1934: 19). The internal physiological responses serve as the biological component of subjectively experienced emotions. Once instincts are modified into impulses, these impulses often include emotional aspects, too. Several of the impulses on Mead's list of human impulses (Mead, 1934: 348f) have emotional components. In Mead's system, human emotions could be traced back through impulses to instincts and seen as modifications of biologically established instincts. Thus, indirectly, "the simple instinctive act . . . lies behind every emotion" (Mead, 1895: 163).

Second, the external components of instinctive acts consist of stereotyped gestures, which are the primary means of communication in animals (Mead, 1934: 14f, 42f, 63f). For example, a dog's snarl communicates anger and a wagging tail communicates friendliness. Humans also display a variety of semistereotyped emotional displays —such as smiles, laughter, blushing, and crying—that reflect inborn response systems, though humans can learn to control and modulate these displays more than animals can. Mead pointed out that normally the internal feelings accompany the external gesture; but a good actor can present the external effects without the internal affect (Mead, 1934: 15-17, 65f; 1938: 293). Conversely, people can have internal feelings but prevent the appearance of the external effects.

Mead used instincts and impulses in his explanations of numerous complex social phenomena, such as the origins of the family, clans, nations, and various types of social organization. These are explained in detail in Chapters 9 and 10.

Inasmuch as instinct theories are no longer accepted in psychology and social psychology, how should modern social scientists deal with Mead's theories of instincts and impulses? Mead's interest in instincts stemmed from his desire to create a unified, nondualistic theory of evolution, physiology, psychology and sociology. Instinct theories were the only theories available at his time for explaining the biologically inherited components of behavior. Even though he was skeptical and critical of the instinct theories from which he had to choose, there were no better alternatives available to him. Given Mead's strong commitment to the scientific method and his anticipation of the constant revision and reconstruction of all scientific theories (Mead, 1917a; 1929a; 1932: 93-118), it is likely that he would have been open to—and supportive of—the modern developments in research and theory on the biosocial bases of behavior. Modern social scientists who wish to further develop and update Mead's empirical model of human behavior and society can benefit by including contemporary biological information in their theories.

* * *

Not only did Mead include evolution, physiology, and instincts in his unified theory, he closely integrated these biological elements with psychological and sociological variables to create a unified, nondualistic model. This type of balanced biosocial theory tends to be considerably more powerful than theories that focus exclusively on either biological factors or social-psychological factors (Hebb, 1972: 127f; Baldwin and Baldwin, 1981; Rossi, 1984).

Mead's commitment to integrating biological data into his unified theory can serve as a model for modern sociologists. Information from the biological sciences can be useful in analyzing many facets of human behavior. Moreover, inattention to biological data and theory has led some sociologists to develop theories that are incompatible with well-documented biological findings. Since Mead's time, there has been significant progress in biological research that is of relevance to sociologists and social psychologists; this work could significantly strengthen the theories in the social sciences.

6

Language and Intelligence

Biology helps explain the foundations of behavior. However, Mead emphasized the need to add numerous social factors to our theoretical systems if we are to deal with the complexities of human thought and action. The first of these social factors that we will investigate is language. Much of human conduct is mediated by language, and the properties of language make possible many of the distinctive qualities of human thought, action, and society. Although Mead recognized the importance of physiological mechanisms in mediating symbolic processes (Mead, 1934: 98-117), he focused most of his attention on the social features of language. Only by living in a social environment in which people use language can the biological individual acquire and use language.

All human societies use language, and through symbolic social interaction they pass the gift of language to each new generation. Of all the things that the child acquires from society, language is one of the most important because, as we will see, it allows the development of the child's biological potential for mental activity, intelligence, sense of self, empathy with others, communication, and many forms of social activity. The structural properties of symbolic communication provide all users of language with powerful tools for social coordination, exchanging ideas, heightened consciousness of meaning, self-awareness, and conscious choice of future actions. This chapter focuses on language as a gift from the social environment (elements b and c in Figure 1; see Chapter 1) and its role in the emergence of conscious and intelligent behavior (h in the figure).[28]

ANIMAL COMMUNICATION

In order to trace the origins of language and explain its role in social and mental processes, Mead began with the instinctual forms of communication seen in lower species and then explained the development of ever more complex forms of communication (Mead, 1904; 1912; 1924-25; 1934). He often compared the communicative acts of dogs, parrots, and other vertebrates with those of humans. The contrast helps clarify the essential properties of communication in lower species and the special qualities of symbolic language that emerged in human evolution.

In order to demonstrate the characteristics of animal communication based on instincts, Mead sometimes gave the example of a confrontation between two hostile dogs (Mead, 1912; 1927a: 142; 1934: 14f, 42f). Two "dogs approaching each other in hostile attitude carry on such a language of gestures. They walk around each other, growling and snapping, and waiting for the opportunity to attack" (Mead, 1934: 14). The displays of each dog provide stimuli that communicate information to the other dog.

> The act of each dog becomes the stimulus to the other dog for his response. . . . The very fact that the dog is ready to attack another becomes a stimulus to the other dog to change his own position or his own attitude. He has no sooner done this than the change of attitude in the second dog in turn causes the first dog to change his attitude. We have here a conversation of gestures [Mead, 1934: 42-43].

In the nonhuman species, each animal adjusts "instinctively" and "without deliberation" in response to the gestures of the other (Mead, 1934: 43).

Darwin had studied the facial, body, and vocal gestures of animals and described them as "expressions of emotions" (Darwin, 1872). According to this view, two snarling dogs would be seen as expressing the internal feelings of anger or hostility. Mead did not deny that there was an emotional component to the instinctive acts seen in animal communication; but he argued that it was incorrect to describe such behavior as merely the expression of emotions (Mead, 1895; 1934: 45). "There are such emotional attitudes which lie back of these [gestural] acts,[29] but these are only part of the whole process that is going on" (Mead, 1934: 45). Mead criticized Darwin for limiting his treatment of gestures to the expression of internal feelings or psychological states (Mead, 1910a; 1914: 33; 1934: 15ff, 42ff). He argued that gestures are the primary means of communication in animals (Mead, 1910a; 1914:

36; 1934: 14ff, 42ff, 63ff). As such, they have important social functions, and hence should not be described as only expressing internal
emotional states. In Mead's theory, the social functions played a
much more important role than the expression of emotions.

In a related vein, Mead was critical of the idea that emotional
gestures are merely an outlet for pent-up feelings. "Excess of energy
seeking outlet [or] the setting free of surplus energy is not the function
of the gesture." "The first function of the [emotional] gesture is the
mutual adjustment of changing social response to changing social
stimulation ... " (Mead, 1910c/1964: 125).

Mead agreed, in part,[30] with Wundt's analysis of animal gestures
and displays: "It was easy for Wundt to show that ... gestures ... did
not at bottom serve the function of expression of the emotions ... "
(Mead, 1934: 44). Rather, gestures must be seen in a larger context, as
"part of the organization of the social act, and highly important elements in that organization" (Mead, 1934: 44). A close examination of
the signals exchanged in animal communication reveals that gestures
are the earliest links in the chain of behaviors that constitute social
acts. "Gestures in their original forms are the first overt phases in
social acts ... " (Mead, 1910c/1964: 123; also see Mead, 1914: 39). As
such, they are stimuli that communicate information about the whole
act. "The term 'gesture' may be identified with these beginnings of
social acts which are stimuli for the response of other [animal] forms"
(Mead, 1934: 43). "Most social stimulation is found in the beginnings
or early stages of social acts which serve as stimuli to other forms
whom these acts would affect" (Mead, 1912/1964: 135). One animal's
gestures indicate to a second individual how the first animal is about
to act. "Back of all gestures, then, lie tendencies to act. Gestures may
be regarded as the beginning of acts" (Mead, 1914: 36). As two animals respond to each other's signals, there is a back and forth exchange of signals, producing a "conversation of gestures" or "conversation of attitudes" (Mead, 1910c/1964: 124; 1912/1964: 136;
1934: 43).

Mead sometimes described gestures as "truncated acts"—that is, as
shortened versions of longer chains of actions (Mead, 1909/1964: 102;
1910a/1964: 109; 1912/1964: 136). The growl of a dog is a shortened
version of the whole aggressive act; and as a truncated version of ag-
gression, it indicates to others what the dog is likely to do next. As
truncated acts, gestures contain information about the *whole* act, including the *future* phases of the act that are likely to follow after the
gesture. When two hostile dogs confront each other, their snarls,
growls, and lunges are the early links in a chain of actions that may

lead to an attack, wounds, and pain. Thus, gestures and displays—as early links in the chain—carry information about the whole chain of events, indicating that a fight may ensue. Because gestures communicate information about the events that are likely to follow, they presage the future, predicting what is likely to happen next. Thus they are predictive stimuli: They provide information that predicts what an individual is likely to do next. In a dog fight, each dog's gestures communicate meaningful information to the other dog because they regularly appear before and therefore predict the next likely events. If one dog bares its teeth and makes a powerful lunge at a second dog, the actions are predictive that it may attack, bite, and inflict a painful wound on the second dog. Thus, as first elements in a chain of action, gestures carry information about the possible outcomes of the whole chain of actions.

Information is valuable in social interaction because it allows individuals to adjust to each other's actions *before* being bitten or groomed or surprised by an unexpected contact. Therefore, animals tend to pay attention to the gestures of others. Referring to gestures, Mead stated, "All of these early stages in animal reaction are of supreme importance as stimuli to social forms [of animals ... and] social forms must become peculiarly sensitive to these earliest overt phases in social acts" (Mead, 1910c/1964: 124). A dog that was not alert or sensitive to the gestures of hostile—or friendly—dogs would be at a disadvantage in social interactions. Through evolutionary and learning processes, animals of most social species have become sensitive and attentive to the gestures of others. "The more perfect the adaptation of the conduct of a social form [of animal], the more readily it would be able to determine its actions by the first indications of an act in another form." "The earlier stages in social acts involve all the beginnings of hostility, wooing and parental care ... " (Mead, 1910c/1964: 123). Because gestures appear at the beginning of a chain of social acts, animals pay attention to gestures and thereby obtain valuable information about the actions that these stimuli indicate may follow.

THE MEANING OF GESTURES

Gestures are meaningful. The meaning of any given gesture lies in the information it carries—in its ability to predict the behavior that is likely to occur next (Mead, 1934: 75-82, 145f). If a gesture is meaningful, "the second organism responds to the gesture of the first as indicating or referring to the completion of the given act" (Mead, 1934:

76-77). If a gesture is regularly followed by specific results, it is a useful predictor of those results. As a consequence, "The gesture stands for a certain resultant of the social act ... so that meaning is given or stated in terms of response" (Mead, 1934: 76). The more reliably the gesture is correlated with a given set of subsequent responses, the more informative and meaningful the stimulus is. Because a dog's wagging tail is almost always predictive of friendly behavior—and rarely associated with aggressive behavior—it carries a more friendly meaning than other gestures that are less reliable predictors of friendly behavior (e.g., jumping or flattening of the ears).

In Mead's analysis, *awareness* of meaning is not necessary for animals to respond to predictive information in gestures. Even though humans can consciously identify the meaning of animal gestures, we should not infer that the animals themselves are "aware" or "conscious" of the meaning. Even though the gestures seen in a dog fight "have ... meaning for us." "We cannot say the animal means it in the sense that he has a reflective determination to attack" (Mead, 1934: 45). Two dogs are not aware of the meaning of the signals that they are exchanging: Meaning can exist without awareness of meaning. "Awareness or consciousness is not necessary to the presence of meaning in the process of social experience." "The mechanism of meaning is thus present in the social act before the emergence of consciousness or awareness of meaning occurs" (Mead, 1934: 77). The mechanism of meaning is present whenever the gestures that appear during the early phases of a chain of actions reliably predict the later phases of the chain of responses.

Even at the human level, action and interaction can be meaningful without the participants' being consciously aware of that meaning. Meaning "is not essentially or primarily ... (a content of mind or consciousness), for it need not be conscious at all, and is not in fact until significant symbols are evolved in the process of human social experience" (Mead, 1934: 80; see also Mead, 1934: 76). Meaning is more primitive than awareness. "[C]onsciousness is an emergent from such [social] behavior; that so far from being a precondition of the social act, the social act is the precondition of it," that is, social interaction is a precondition of consciousness (Mead, 1934: 18).

For Mead, meaning is "objectively there" in the social interaction—and the meaningful information is often used by the interactants—even if no one is aware of it (Mead, 1934: 76). After observing that dogs with wagging tails usually turn out to be friendly, we can identify, through objective data alone, that the wagging tail is a gesture with a friendly meaning. Dogs obviously respond to the tail-wag as a friendly gesture, too, even though they are not conscious of its meaning the way we are. Meaning is visible in the overt behavior of animals (including humans) whenever gestures serve as predictive stimuli that carry reliable information about the actions that are likely to follow. "Meaning is thus a development of something objectively there[31] as a relation between certain phases of the social act; it is not a psychical addition to that act and it is not an 'idea' as traditionally conceived" (Mead, 1934: 76).

Mead explained that meaning of social gestures can be analyzed in terms of a triad of events (Mead, 1934: 75-82, 145f): the relationship between (1) a first individual's gesture, (2) a second individual's response, and (3) the consequences of the interaction. "The logical structure of meaning ... is to be found in the threefold relationship of gesture to adjustive response and to the resultant of the given social act" (Mead, 1934: 80). We will label this the "G-R-C triad" to stand for the "relation of the *gesture* of one organism to the adjustive *response* of another organism...to the *completion* of the given act... " (Mead, 1934: 76; emphasis added). If an infant monkey gives a "caw" call (G), its mother comes (R), and the infant climbs onto the mother for contact and nursing (C), the meaning of the "caw" call can be established: It is a signal for mother to come and provide nurturance. "The basis of meaning is thus objectively there in social conduct ... " (Mead, 1934: 80), and the meaning of a gesture can be determined by objective observations on the G-R-C triad (or triads)[32] in which the gesture occurs.

The meaning of human gestures can be evaluated objectively, too. If we visit a foreign country and see someone use a strange hand gesture, we would not immediately know its meaning. However, if we observed several instances in which one person gave the gesture to another, the second person yelled back and the two got into a fight, we could conclude that the gesture carried a hostile meaning. "This threefold or triadic relation between gesture, adjustive response, and resultant of the social act . . . is the basis of meaning . . . " (Mead, 1934: 80).

THE VOCAL GESTURE

Although all types of gestures are capable of having meaning and communicating information to other individuals, only certain forms of gestures can communicate the same meaning to *both* the sender and receiver. For reasons that will soon become clear, Mead was especially interested in gestures that carry the same meaning to both the individual who gives them and the individual who perceives them. "Our interest is in finding gestures which can affect the individual that is responsible for them in the same manner as that in which they affect other individuals" (Mead, 1924-25/1964: 287).

In nonhuman animals, the bodily movements and postures of one animal are gestures that communicate meaning to others, but *not* to the individual who made the gestures. When an angry dog bares its teeth at another, it does not see its own gesture the way the other dog sees it. "The stimulus in the attitude of one dog is not to call out the response in itself that it calls out in the other" (Mead, 1934: 63). When a dog makes facial or body gestures that communicate meaningful information to others, it cannot perceive those gestures and their meanings itself because it cannot see its own body the way others do.

In contrast to body movements and postures, the vocal gesture is perceived much the same by the sender and the receiver. This phenomenon and its importance are most conspicuous when we compare the vocal and nonvocal gestures used by humans.[33] When a person uses a vocal gesture—"Pull up a chair, and let's have a friendly chat"—both the speaker and the listener hear the same words and understand the same meanings. "The vocal gesture is ... one that assails our ears who make it in the same physiological fashion as that in which it affects others. We hear our own vocal gestures as others hear them" (Mead, 1924-25/1964: 287; see also Mead, 1922/1964: 243). In some cases, the words even call up similar overt responses in the speaker and listener: If you ask someone to pull up a chair and chat, both of you may move a chair into a good position, and both of you will be inclined to begin the conversation in a friendly, casual manner.[34] "The importance, then, of the vocal stimulus lies in this fact that the individual can hear what he says and in hearing what he says is tending to respond as the other person responds" (Mead, 1934: 69-70). Thus, there is a special quality to the vocal gesture: It has the potential to communicate the same meaning to both the speaker and the listener.

> It is this which gives such peculiar importance to the vocal gesture: it is one of those social stimuli which affect the form that makes it in the same fashion that it affects the form when made by another. That is, we can hear ourselves talking, and the import of what we say is the same to ourselves that it is to others [Mead, 1934: 62].

Our facial gestures, body postures, blushing, blanching, and other nonvocal gestures are quite different from our vocal gestures, because we cannot see the nonvocal gestures the same as others can. When you smile at another person, you do not see the facial display that the other person sees. Although you feel sensations from the internal muscular actions involved in making the facial gesture, these sensations are extremely different from the stimulus pattern perceived by the other person. This is not true of the vocal gesture: "While one feels but imperfectly the value of his own facial expression or bodily attitude for another, his ear reveals to him his own vocal gesture in the same form that it assumes to his neighbor" (Mead, 1912/1964: 136-137). (Our ability to see hand gestures as others do is discussed in the following section.)

Because the internal feelings that accompany nonvocal gestures do not give us much information about the effect of those gestures on others, actors use mirrors to see how different facial expressions appear to others. This helps them learn how to gain conscious control over various nonvocal gestures (Mead, 1934: 65f). The actor "gets a response which reveals to him how he looks by continually using a mirror" (Mead, 1934: 65). "If we exclude vocal gestures, it is only by the use of the mirror that one could reach the position where he responds to his own gestures as other people respond" (Mead, 1934: 66).

The ease with which people can respond to their own vocal gestures much as others do—without special training with mirrors, videotapes, and so forth—allows us to be much more *aware* of our vocal gestures than we are of other types of gestures.

> The vocal gesture . . . has an importance which no other gesture has. We cannot see ourselves when our face assumes a certain expression. If we hear ourselves speak we are more apt to pay attention. One hears himself when he is irritated using a tone that is of an irritable quality, and so catches himself. But in the facial expression of irritation the stimulus is not one that calls out an expression in the individual which it calls out in the other. One is more apt to catch himself up and control himself in the vocal gesture than in the expression of the countenance [Mead, 1934: 65].

Thus, vocal gestures are much more likely than nonvocal gestures to give us self-awareness and an awareness of the way that others perceive our actions. This, in turn, facilitates self-control and the self-adjustment needed for subtle social coordination with others.

SIGNIFICANT SYMBOLS

So far, we have established that it is easier to perceive vocal gestures the way that other people perceive them than it is to perceive most nonvocal gestures as others do. When vocal gestures are used, the sender and the receiver hear the same stimuli. However, do they make the same responses to these stimuli? Not necessarily. Do vocal gestures communicate the same meaning to the sender and the receiver? Not always.

The mere fact that vocal gestures are heard in the same way by sender and receiver does not guarantee that both individuals will respond to them in the same manner or find the same meaning in them. Mead pointed out that the vocal gestures of nonhuman animals usually call up different responses in the sender and the receiver. Most nonhuman animals have a repertoire of vocal gestures that are used in social situations. When dogs bark, birds sing, or lions roar, the animals hear their own vocal gestures. However, the mere fact that the sender hears the same vocal gesture that the listener hears does not guarantee that the sender will *respond* to the vocal gesture the same way the listener does. "The lion does not appreciably frighten itself by its roar. The roar has an effect of frightening the animal he is attacking, and it has also the character of a challenge under certain conditions" (Mead, 1934: 63-64). Both the lion and the listener hear the roar, but the sound does not call up the same responses in the lion and in the listener.

When humans evolved to the point where they began to use language, they gained access to a type of vocal gesture[35] that usually calls up the same response in the speaker and listener—if both people use the same language, and their words have standardized usages. "In a human society, a language gesture is a stimulus that reverberates and calls out the same attitude in the individual who makes it as it does in others who respond to it; we hear what we say to others as well as what others say to us" (Mead, 1927a: 136). The words "pull up a chair," have the same meaning for all people who speak English. Therefore, when a speaker utters these words, the words have the same meanings for both the speaker and the listener. When a gesture calls up the same meanings in both the speaker and the listener, Mead defined it as a "significant gesture," as it has the same significance to both people (Mead, 1924-25/1964: 288; 1927a: 136; 1932: 189; 1934: 45ff, 67). In the case of language—where the vocal gesture is a symbol—the significant gesture is called a "significant symbol." "Gestures become significant symbols when they implicitly arouse in an individual making them the same responses which they explicitly arouse, or are supposed to arouse, in other individuals, the individuals to whom they are addressed ... " (Mead, 1934: 47).

Not all human vocal gestures and symbols are significant. If one person graciously says, "Bitte, nehmen Sie Platz," and the listener shows no sign of understanding, it may be that the listener does not understand German. In that case, the vocal gesture does not have the same significance for the speaker and listener. When vocal gestures or symbols do not communicate the same meaning to both speaker and listener, Mead defined them as "non-significant," indicating that they do not have the same significance to both people (Mead, 1934: 81). (However, the very same symbols—"Bitte, nehmen Sie Platz"—can be significant symbols for any two people who know that the words are a polite invitation to have a seat.)

In the nonhuman animals, gestures are typically nonsignificant.[36] The conversation of gestures between two snarling dogs is not significant, because the growl of one dog does not have the same meaning to the sender and the receiver (Mead, 1924-25/1964: 286; 1934: 63f). "Birds tend to sing to themselves, babies to talk to themselves. The sounds they make are stimuli to make other sounds" (Mead, 1934: 65). However, the vocalization of birds and babies are not significant because they do not call up the same response in the sender and the listener. "The hunting dog points to the hidden bird. The lost lamb that bleats, and the child that cries each points himself out to his mother. All of these gestures, to the intelligent observer, are significant symbols, but they are none of them significant to the forms that make them" (Mead, 1922/1964: 243f), because the sender does not perceive the same meaning that the receiver does.

In any language, the commonly used vocal gestures are usually significant symbols because these words typically have the same meaning for all people who speak that language. "That is fundamental for any language; if it is going to be language one has to understand what he is saying, has to affect himself as he affects others" (Mead, 1934: 75). Of course, words, like all gestures, are meaningful only if they are predictive stimuli that indicate the result of the acts that they presage. "It is, then, this mechanism of indication, showing the final result of the act in the present activity, that gives importance to language and communication" (Mead, 1927a: 159).

Although Mead repeatedly stated that a symbol must have the *same* meaning to the speaker and listener to be a significant symbol (Mead, 1922; 1924-25/1964: 286ff; 1927a: 136, 160f; 1934: 46f, 67, 147ff, 161, 269, 327), it is clear that he did not assume that people would have *identical* responses to any given significant symbol. First, Mead recognized that each individual is unique (Mead, 1914: 61f; 1934: 201f, 324, 326ff; 1936: 415ff);[37] hence each will have at least slightly different responses to any given significant symbol. Because each individual has had different past experiences and views the world from a different perspective (Mead, 1924-25/1964: 276; 1934: 201; 1936: 415ff), each tends to understand things in at least somewhat different ways. Although two individuals may have *approximately* the same response to a given significant symbol, absolutely identical responses are unlikely. For example, a word such as "dog" can call up different responses in different people. "There is a whole series of possible responses. There are certain types of these responses which are in all of us, and there are others which *vary with the individuals,* but there is always an organization of the responses which can be called out by the term 'dog'" (Mead, 1934: 71, emphasis added). It is the similarity of organization that allows two people to understand the word "dog" in a similar manner. However, each person's unique experiences with dogs introduces variability into different people's responses to the word. Small variations may have no noticeable effect on the success of communication; but large variations can interfere with effective communication and social coordination. When people's responses to a symbol become too different, the symbol is not a significant symbol for them.

As it is clear that people are different and cannot have absolutely identical responses to any given symbol, what did Mead mean when he repeatedly stated that people must have the *same* response to a symbol for it to be significant? It has been suggested (Anonymous, ca. 1925/1982) that Mead meant that people's responses to significant symbols must be "functionally the same" rather than absolutely the same or perfectly identical. As long as a word calls up responses that have the same functions for two different people, we can say that it has the same general meaning. The words "pull up a chair" can lead to a large variety of responses, but all those that function to bring a chair close enough for easy conversation are similar enough to be grouped in the same "class of acts" (Anonymous, ca. 1925/1982: 203). Hence they are *"behaviorally* the same" (Anonymous, ca. 1925/1982: 201).[38] Even though there may be considerable variability in the physical responses performed, there is a functional identity.

This interpretation is completely compatible with Mead's descriptions of his psychology as a form of "functional psychology" (Mead, 1903/1964: 54f; 1910a/1964: 270; 1938: 630). By this term, Mead meant that behavioral and mental processes should be evaluated according to their function within the larger social and life processes. As long as the words "pull up a chair" call up functionally similar responses—functioning to create proximity for a comfortable conversation—the responses can be considered "functionally the same," even though no two people carry out the act in identical manners.

There is a second way in which we need to qualify the statement that significant symbols call up the *same* response in the speaker and listener. Although significant symbols usually call up functionally similar meanings and actions, they can elicit very different emotional responses. Mead stated that words can affect people in two ways: They can both "convey a certain meaning" and elicit an "emotional throb" (Mead, 1934: 75). The emotional responses of different individuals to any given significant symbol are often quite different (Mead, 1934: 147f). When parents tell their teenager that the teen must be home by an early hour on date nights, the teen may understand the intellectual meaning of the parents' words much the same as they do, but the teen is likely to have quite different emotional responses to those words than the parents have. Mead traced the differences in the emotional responses of the speaker and listener to "the natural function of language...." "We do not normally use language stimuli to call out in ourselves the emotional response which we are calling out in others" (Mead, 1934: 148). For example, when "one tries to bully somebody else, he is not trying to bully himself" (Mead, 1934: 147). The bully's aggressive words and accusations may heighten his own emotions of anger, while eliciting feelings of fear or hatred in the other person. Nevertheless, the bully's words are also likely to have the same intellectual meaning for both people.

Although language often does not elicit the same emotions in the speaker and listener, Mead identified situations in which a speaker will arouse the same emotions in self as in others. For example, actors and poets sometimes do this (Mead, 1934: 147f). A poet who wants to convey emotions of joy or wonder will experiment with various words and "test his results in himself by seeing whether these words do call out in him the [emotional] response he wants to call out in others" (Mead, 1934: 148). The effect is not limited to actors and poets. Whenever people try to vividly communicate their emotions to others, they are prone to select words that elicit the same emotions in both themselves and others, in order to strike a "responsive chord." In addition, there are times when a person's words naturally have similar effects on both speaker and listener. For example, "a man who calls 'fire' would be able to call out in himself the reaction he calls out in the other ... [i.e, a] sense of terror" (Mead, 1934: 190).

Although Mead emphasized the importance of the vocal gesture as the basic form of language, he also recognized that sign languages and writing are all legitimate forms of communication, too. Because the sender can *see* his or her hand signs or written words much as the receiver can, these types of nonvocal gestures have the most important property of the vocal gesture: Both sender and receiver can *respond* to the signed word or written word in much the same manner (Mead, 1924-25/1964: 287; 1934: 67f). However, Mead focused less attention on these forms of communication because "such symbols have all been developed out of the specific vocal gesture ... " (Mead, 1934:

67-68). He considered sign language and writing as secondary modes of communication, derivatives of vocal language. "It has been the vocal gesture that has preeminently provided the medium of social organization in human society" (Mead, 1924-25/1964: 287).

CONVERSATION AND INNER CONVERSATION

Without significant symbols, people would not be able to carry on conversations and understand each other. One person's words— "Guritz gyestix remzit omoraz"—would be meaningless to others; and there would be no communication. Only through significant symbols that have similar meanings for all the users of a given language do people gain the ability to communicate, share ideas, and coordinate meaningful behavior. Perfect communication does not exist (Mead, 1934: 325-328); but even our imperfect communication is vastly superior to the exchange of meaningless vocal gestures such as "Guritz gyestix remzit omoraz."

When we use significant symbols with others, we hear our own words and the sounds call up in ourselves ideas that are similar to the ideas that the words call up in others. "But it is not necessary that we should talk to another to have these ideas. We can talk to ourselves, and this we do in the inner forum of what we call thought" (Mead, 1924-25/1964: 288). Language gives us not only the ability to carry out conversations with others, but also the ability to carry out internal conversations in our own heads. The individual "talks to himself as he talks to others and in keeping up this conversation in the inner forum constitutes the field which is called that of mind" (Mead, 1922/1964: 243). "The mechanism of thought, insofar as thought uses symbols which are used in social intercourse, is but an inner conversation" (Mead, 1913/1964: 146).

The inner conversation is conducted with the same significant symbols used in social communication. "Only in terms of gestures as significant symbols is the existence of mind or intelligence possible; for only in terms of gestures which are significant symbols can thinking—which is simply an internalized or implicit conversation of the individual with himself by means of such gestures—take place" (Mead, 1934: 47). Thus, mind is an internalized form of symbolic social interaction. "The internalization in our experience of the external conversations of gestures which we carry on with other individuals in the social process is the essence of thinking ... " (Mead, 1934: 47).

Because the thinker is using significant symbols that have the same meanings for both self and others, the thinker's inner conversation is socially meaningful and useful. After mentally developing some interesting ideas through an inner conversation, the thinker can share the same words that were used in private thought to communicate those ideas with others. Because the ideas are couched in significant symbols, the listener can understand the words, ideas, and meanings that the speaker had first experienced in the privacy of his or her own mind. Because we think with significant symbols, we can share our ideas with others and have meaningful exchanges of thoughts. It is clear that Mead's model of mind and thought is a social model: It does not suggest the isolation and solipsism that dualistic and individualistic theories do.[39]

The inner conversation we carry out in our heads can be with ourselves, with specific people we know, with imaginary people, or with an imaginary other person that Mead called the "generalized other" (Mead, 1934: 154ff). The generalized other—which is described in greater detail in Chapter 7—is basically a composite of all sorts of people. When we are wondering what other people "in general" would think and ask ourselves, "What would *they* think?" we are asking what the generalized other would think. If we hear an answer to the question, it is the generalized other who is speaking. No matter who the speakers are in the inner conversation, they almost always use significant symbols, which are both socially and personally meaningful. It is this meaningful inner conversation of significant symbols that gives rise to the higher forms of consciousness seen in humans (Mead, 1914: 43ff; 1934: 80, 132).

CONSCIOUSNESS

Mead recognized that consciousness exists in different degrees in different species (Mead, 1907; 1924-25/1964: 273ff; 1932: 68ff). In essence, there are various levels of consciousness and awareness, ranging from simple feelings in primitive animals to increasingly sophisticated perceptual consciousness in advanced species, to abstract and symbolic consciousness in humans. "There can be no hard and fast line drawn between such perceptual consciousness and the more abstracted processes of so-called reasoning" (Mead, 1907/1964: 81).

Perceptual consciousness is the most basic form of consciousness (Mead, 1922; 1934: 330ff). Even lower species are conscious of feelings and sensations that arise from the inputs to their sensory systems, though each species has different sensory systems and therefore different perceptual worlds (Mead, 1924-25/1964: 277; 1934: 215, 245). Even within a species, individuals have different perceptual consciousness if they "slice" the world from different perspectives (Mead, 1924-25/1964: 276). In addition, the contents of perceptual consciousness depend on which sensory input channels are open. "With the eyes shut we can say we are no longer conscious of visual objects." "A general anesthetic shuts out all objects" from consciousness (Mead, 1922/1964: 247).

Consciousness of meaning is a special type of consciousness that emerged when humans evolved to the point of using language and carrying out an inner conversation of significant symbols (Mead, 1914: 43ff; 1934: 80). Because significant symbols are meaningful gestures, an inner conversation with such symbols heightens our consciousness of meaning. "In language, what we have reached is the consciousness of meaning attached to a gesture" (Mead, 1914: 43). Consciousness of meaning can take various forms when we use the words of our inner conversation to describe events and things, to evaluate problematic situations and possible solutions, to carry out scientific investigations, to deal with ethical and aesthetic questions, and so forth (Mead, 1900; 1936). It is this consciousness of meaning—and the advanced forms of behavior that it allows—that makes humans so different from the other species.

One of the most automatic ways in which we become conscious of meaning occurs when we verbally describe things or events in our environment, or inside our bodies. Because significant symbols call up meanings, the use of these symbols to describe things or events leads to a heightened awareness of the meanings that are indicated by our symbols. "Mentality on our approach simply comes in when the organism is able to point out meanings to others and to himself. This is the point at which mind appears, or if you like, emerges" (Mead, 1934: 132). For example, both humans and other animals can have simple perceptual awareness of the presence of a hammer on a table. However, humans can verbally label or describe the hammer, and the use of significant symbols makes us aware of the meaning of the hammer. Because the results of an act are especially crucial in establishing its meaning, "the ultimate act of driving a nail is for us the meaning of the hammer" (Mead, 1927a: 130). Because significant symbols make us conscious of meaning, verbal descriptions provide more awareness than can simple perceptual consciousness alone. "We do not have the consciousness of meaning except when we can indicate the stimuli, the symbols, to ourselves" (Mead, 1914: 44).

Social awareness appears for similar reasons. For example, all social interaction involves countless nonverbal cues: body movements, posture, hand gestures, facial expressions, and the amount of distance people maintain between each other. Even though these cues enter everyone's perceptual consciousness, most people are not consciously aware of the meaning of the more subtle nonverbal cues that constantly are present in social interaction. When they first read an article or hear a lecture that explains the meaning of subtle social cues, they learn to describe these social actions with significant symbols. At that time, most people experience an "Ah-Ha!" effect—a sudden heightened awareness of these social cues and their meanings. "We find that our consciousness of meaning has passed over in part into articulate speech—a readiness to describe an object corresponds to our consciousness of what it is" (Mead, 1914: 44-45).

REFLECTIVE INTELLIGENCE

Although verbal description produces a consciousness of meaning, there is a higher form of consciousness that arises from the use of significant symbols: Mead called it "reflective consciousness" or "reflective intelligence."[40] People experience this form of consciousness whenever they confront problems and use an inner conversation of significant symbols to work toward a solution. Mead gave the following example: "A man walking across country comes upon a chasm which he cannot jump. He wants to go ahead but the chasm prevents this tendency from being carried out." "When he stops, mind, we say, is freed" (Mead, 1934: 122). Namely, "he notes all the possibilities of getting across. He can hold onto them by means of symbols, and relate them to each other so that he can get a final action" (Mead, 1934: 123). By using significant symbols to "hold onto" each of the various possible solutions and evaluate its feasibility, the person gains heightened[41] awareness of the meaning of his situation and his choices for future action.

Mead's basic assumption[42] was that "all reflective thought arises out of real problems present in immediate experience, and is occupied entirely with the solution of these problems or their attempted solution ... [and] ... this solution finally is found in the possibility of continuing the activity, that has been stopped, along new or old lines ... " (Mead, 1900/1964: 7). Problems and conflicts block the completion of the act and cause us to seek solutions. "First of all, there is that checking of activity which is essential to reflective consciousness; the necessity for adjustment to the changed situation." "If we are in doubt, we have several tendencies to respond, which mutually check one another" (Mead, 1914: 45). Because each response tendency checks and inhibits the other, our overt action is stopped long enough that we can cognitively reflect on and become aware of the various responses available to us. Consciousness appears in "a situation in which action has started but has been stopped and cannot go on for the time being, and we are looking for the symbols that will enable us to go ahead, which will serve as stimuli to set free the activity and to enable us to complete the action" (Mead, 1914: 44). We use the inner conversation to sort through all the symbols that call up images (see Chapter 5) of possible solutions to the problem that has blocked our action. "The process of exercising intelligence is the process of delaying, organizing, and selecting a response or reaction to the stimuli of the given environmental situation" (Mead, 1934: 100). Because it is done with significant symbols, reflective intelligence makes us aware of the meaning of our situation and of our possible future actions.

Mead did not claim that all human acts were conscious. "Only portions of the response appear in consciousness as such" (Mead, 1934: 22-23). "Subconsciousness is frequently part of our conduct. Stimuli occur in that field, the act follows, but there is no precept. [For consciousness,] there must be conflict. This results in inhibition, the throwing up in consciousness of past experience" (Mead, 1914: 31). When there are no conflicts and no problems to block our actions, conduct is often done without consciousness. When someone stops us on the street and asks for directions, we may point in the direction that the person needs to go while answering. The habitual response of pointing is so natural and easy that we may not be consciously aware that we are pointing as we answer the question. However, if the person says that she is blind and cannot see the direction we are pointing, we suddenly become very aware of our pointing; it is totally inappropriate in this situation. The old habitual response no longer works. We have failed to communicate. Our habitual action is blocked and we pause. It is in this pause that the process of reflective intelligence is called into operation. At this point, we are likely to reflect on the different alternatives that are available for resolving the problem. There are several possibilities: We could take the blind person to her destination, or verbally describe the route needed for her to get there, or ask a passerby who is walking in the correct direction to accompany the blind person, or consider yet other options. Merely thinking about carrying out each alternative leads to images of the whole series of actions involved in each alternative, along with its outcomes for both the blind person and ourself.

Reflective consciousness evaluates possible future events based on past experience. "Intelligence is essentially the ability to solve the problems of present behavior in terms of its possible future consequences as implicated on the basis of past experience—the ability, that is, to solve the problems of present behavior in the light of, or by reference to, both the past and the future; it involves both memory and foresight" (Mead, 1934: 100).

The Future. Because all gestures are predictive stimuli, they carry information about the future—about the results of the acts they presage. Therefore, when we use significant symbols to reflect on possible solutions to problems, they call up images of the possible future outcomes of each act. "When ... we speak of reflective conduct we very definitely refer to the presence of the future in terms of ideas. The intelligent man ... presents to himself what is going to happen." "It is this picture ... of what the future is to be ... that is the characteristic of human intelligence" (Mead, 1934: 119).

The significant symbol is the stimulus that allows us to call up this awareness of the future. "One gets the response into experience before the response is overtly carried out through indicating and emphasizing the stimulus that instigates it" (Mead, 1934: 120). The significant symbol calls up images of the whole act: "This imagery gives us the result of the act before we carry it out" (Mead, 1914: 29). Thus, future consequences can affect current behavior. "Our conduct is made up of a series of steps which follow each other, and the later steps may be already started and influence the earlier ones. The thing we are going to do is playing back on what we are doing now" (Mead, 1934: 71).[43]

Mead traced our power of choice to the ability to respond to the later parts of the act during the early stages of the act. "It is the ability of later responses to play back into immediate responses that gives us our flexibility and power of choice" (Mead, 1927a: 158). "The field of the control of present behavior [is] in terms of its future consequences, or in terms of future behavior ... " (Mead, 1934: 118). Once we have reviewed all of our possible future behaviors in the inner conversation, we can compare the future consequences of each alternative and determine which is most suitable. The goal is to act "in such a way as to make possible the most adequate and harmonious solution ... of the given environmental problem" (Mead, 1934: 98).

The Past. All expectations about future events are based on past happenings: either in the evolutionary past of the species or the developmental past of the individual. Nonhuman animals often act in ways that assure desirable future results, but they do not use reflective intelligence. Mead presented a "Darwinian explanation" to show how animals evolved to respond in ways that produce adaptive future consequences, without any awareness of the future (Mead, 1934: 118f). "The forms whose conduct does insure the future will naturally survive" even though the animal has no awareness of future as such (Mead, 1934: 119).

Although some human instincts and impulses orient us toward adaptive future consequences, most future-oriented behavior in humans results from the use of images, symbols, or reflective intelligence that help us predict future events based on our past experience. We expect a growling dog to be dangerous because in the past this canine gesture has been a good predictor that a dog may be aggressive. We expect the words "I love you" to presage a caring interaction if, in the past, these significant symbols have been good predictors of caring interaction. Reflective intelligence is also based on past experience (Mead, 1934: 100). When we confront a problem, "this results in inhibition, the throwing up in consciousness of past experience" (Mead, 1914: 31). We reflect on our past responses—and their outcomes—in similar situations. "There is imagery of a past experience which has been carried out under the same or similar stimulation" (Mead, 1914: 29). The more similar our present situation is to past situations that we have experienced, the more likely we are to have knowledge about the future outcomes that we can expect in the present situation. In contrast, if we are in a situation that is extremely different from anything we have ever experienced in the past, we may find it very difficult to predict the future outcomes of our current actions. Even with much relevant past experience, there is no guarantee that our predictions about the future will be accurate.

In fact, our conceptions of the past and future are continually changing (Mead, 1929a; 1929b; 1932: 7-9, 24-31). The past and future exist for us only as images and symbolic accounts; and these are always open to change as new events occur and we have new experiences. For example, our images and accounts of a well-remembered childhood event may be altered when we learn that our mother and father had been going through a difficult crisis at the time and that they had sheltered us from that fact. This new information changes our perception of the past. Thoughts about the future also change as each day brings new experiences. Because unexpected events are always happening (Mead, 1899; 1929a; 1929b; 1932; 1936: 290f, 405-417), they continually alter our images and accounts of both the past and the future. In essence, the past and future are always hypothetical (Mead, 1932: 21, 48).

Because our knowledge of the past and future is in constant flux, it is difficult to plan fully for future events. Therefore, the most careful application of reflective intelligence cannot completely predict the future or guarantee perfectly adaptive decisions. Nevertheless, reflective intelligence—especially as practiced scientifically—is the best method we have for assessing the future and planning both personal and social actions (Mead, 1899; 1917a, 1923; 1932; 1936).

* * *

This chapter summarized Mead's theory of the structure and properties of the communicative stimuli used by nonhuman animals and humans. Mead emphasized the importance of the vocal gesture because the individual who sends a vocal gesture can perceive that vocal signal much the same as the listener does. However, hearing the same sound that others hear does not guarantee that the sender will respond to it or understand its meaning the same way the listener does. Only when humans evolved the biological mechanisms for language and developed significant symbols did our species acquire the type of vocal gesture that can have the same meaning for the speaker and listener. Significant symbols allow people to communicate more effectively than can other species *and* to carry out inner conversations with themselves in the privacy of their own heads. The inner conversation, in turn, gives rise to higher levels of consciousness about the past, present, and future. It also provides the mechanism for the reflective intelligence by which we can evaluate our future actions and select the ones that seem most suitable.

Language played a central role in Mead's theory. Not only does language make possible some of the most distinctive forms of behavior seen in our species—symbolic communication, the inner conversation of the mind, and reflective intelligence—it is central to the development of a self-concept, self-control, role-taking, empathy, and numerous other social psychological phenomena. It is also the most important vehicle for transmitting social customs, coordinating social processes, and implementing social change. In subsequent chapters, it will become increasingly clear that language is of enormous importance in mediating countless forms of micro and macro social processes.

7

Socialization and Role Taking

This chapter focuses on the socialization process,[44] especially its early phases, and explains the different types of role taking that emerge with the onset of language use, role play, and games. Early in life, infants interact primarily with their families, the micro social environment (b in Figure 1; see Chapter 1). However, as children gain increasing skill and competence, they expand their range of interaction to ever larger spheres of the environment, gaining increasing contact with macro social and physical environments (c and d in Figure 1).

Although part of early socialization involves the parents' explicitly training and instructing the child (arrow e in Figure 1), the socialization process is not merely something that society *does* to the child. The child is not a passive receptacle, waiting to be filled with social contents. Rather, children actively investigate and interact with their social and physical worlds (arrows i, j, and k), acquiring information from the interaction of their own behavior and the environment (arrows e, f, and g). Through this interaction, children develop increasingly sophisticated mental and behavioral capacities (h in Figure 1).

"THE CHILD'S WORLD IS A SOCIAL WORLD"

For several reasons, Mead described the child's world as a social world (Mead, 1927a: 140). The infant is born into a social environment and is highly dependent on the parents and other caretakers for survival. The infant has a small repertoire of inborn behaviors, or "inherited coordinations, but they are few and simple" (Mead, 1927a: 140).[45] The inborn responses are too primitive to allow babies to cope

by themselves with the physical environment. They rely almost completely on their caretakers to mediate their interactions with the
physical environment. "The child must act with reference to the
[social] structure that protects and supports him; he lives in a social
medium, and through this he comes into relationship with his physical
environment. He does not come into relationship with the physical
world directly" (Mead, 1927a: 140). Thus, for Mead the physical environment is of secondary importance to the micro social environment
in explaining the early development and socialization of the young
infant.

Much of the infant's early behavior consists of random, undif-
ferentiated movements. Over time, these gradually become organized
into coordinated response patterns. According to Mead, this occurs
largely under the influence of social interaction, though he recognized
the role of maturational variables, too. "The organization of the random movements is the occupation of the child, and this occurs in the
social structure" (Mead, 1927a: 140). "In infancy essential processes
are mediated by the group around the infant, which carries out the
presence actually conditioning his life. In this process there are random acts in the course of organization, ripening of coordinations in
the central nervous system, and the development of synapses" (Mead,
1927a: 141).

Mead observed that many of the infant's inborn responses are
social in nature, as can be seen by looking at the stimuli that release
them. "If there are instincts in humans, as in animals, they lie in the
social environment, for the stimuli to which the child responds are
there" (Mead, 1927a: 140). "To the young child the frowns and smiles
of those about him ... are at first simply stimulation that call out instinctive responses of his own appropriate to these gestures. He cries
or laughs, he moves toward his mother, or stretches out his arms"
(Mead, 1912/1964: 137). The inborn responses to social stimuli allow
babies to coordinate with others before they have gained enough personal experience to know how to organize their own actions. "The
baby withdraws from persons with certain expressions of countenance
without any previous experience of that sort" (Mead, 1914: 42).
"Whether we can refer to this attitude [of the infant] as instinctive or
not, there is no question that the young child responds readily long
before his own experience can help him. The tone of voice and the expression of the countenance are particularly effective in bringing
about certain responses" (Mead, 1914: 38).

Not only does the infant respond to the social cues of others, the infant's inborn responses serve as meaningful cues for others. Parents

understand the meaning of their baby's smile or cry because they see the triadic relationship between the infant's inborn gesture, the parental response to it, and the consequences of this interaction—that is, they see the G-R-C triad (of gesture-response-consequences) on which meaning is based. For example, the meaning of the baby's cry is visible in the following G-R-C triads. If the infant cries and the parents do not go to the infant's aid, there will be prolonged crying. However, if the baby cries and the parents come and change the diapers, the child will become quieter. These G-R-C triads make clear that the cry means that the child needs help. All the infant's gestures can be understood in terms of such G-R-C triads, though cries are more easily understood than some of the infant's more subtle or variable gestures.

The baby's inborn gestures begin social acts that the infant cannot complete without assistance from others; and normally the parents complete the acts. The infant "gets a response from those around him, and it is they who actually carry out or complete his act. In other words, he relies on others to complete his acts for him" (Mead, 1927a: 141). For example, the infant's cry indicates a need for help, and adults respond by coming to the child and changing the diapers.

Through repeated social interaction, children gain experience with the G-R-C triads involving both the parents' and their own gestures, and gradually become aware of the meanings of these social gestures. When the parents respond to a child's own gestures and actions, "the child has the material out of which he builds up the social objects that form the most important part of his environment" (Mead, 1912/1964: 137). Gradually, the child develops ever clearer images of the caretakers as "social objects"[46] with distinctive characteristics and personalities. Eventually, the child becomes "confident that he recognizes the different members of the group about him. He acts then with confidence toward them since their gestures have come to have meaning for him. His own response to their stimulations and its consequences are there to interpret the facial expressions and attitudes of body and tones of voice" (Mead, 1912/1964: 137-138). Their gestures are meaningful because the child has experienced the G-R-C triads indicated by those gestures and built up mental images of the responses indicated by them.

Developing images and awareness of mother and father is among the first steps for the infant to become social *and* later to acquire an awareness of self. In numerous places, Mead emphasized that it is only after children develop a clear perception of other individuals as personalities and selves that they can understand and develop awareness of their own actions and selves (Mead, 1910a; 1912/1964: 138f; 1914: 42, 53-56; 1927a: 107, 156).

AWARENESS OF PHYSICAL OBJECTS

Although Mead viewed the child's world as primarily a social world, he did not neglect the child's interaction with the physical environment and the ways in which the child develops increasing awareness of physical objects (Mead, 1927a: 140). The meaning of objects is derived from the results of contacting, manipulating, and using them.[47] For example, the meaning of a spade is in its use: "For a child, the spade is something to dig with" (Mead, 1927a: 132). Children gain awareness of the meaning of objects by watching their parents and from first-hand experience.

Parents help the child learn the meaning of things by demonstrating their use. For example, they help their infant learn the use and meaning of a ball by rolling the ball up to the child or moving the child's hand to hit and roll the ball. "The adult, in this process, is constantly indicating to the child the results of his own motions: the ball is something to get hold of and throw. Things done with the object are referred to the child, so that when the child plays he will see the end and learn to pick out the object's ultimate use" (Mead, 1927a: 134). The child does not know what a ball is at first, but when the parents roll it and demonstrate its "ultimate use," the child sees the results and gains awareness of the meaning of balls—things to roll, play with, and watch.

Preverbal children clearly show that they are aware of the meanings of objects in their environment. Balls, rattles, stuffed animals, and other toys become meaningful stimuli to young children, though of course they do not understand the meaning of stereo equipment, calculators, or other objects that they cannot use. The objects that are most meaningful to an infant are those that the infant can contact and use enough to gain an understanding of their ultimate use.

Not only do children learn from watching their parents' actions, they are active in seeking out their own experience with physical objects.[48] Both Dewey (1896) and Mead (1900, 1903) gave the example of a young child's responses when first seeing a candle flame. Before touching the flame, the child has little sense of the meaning of this pretty, colorful stimulus.[49] The flickering light is merely "a bright moving object" (Mead, 1900/1964: 13): It is a sensuous experience in the perceptual consciousness, but it is devoid of meaning. However, once the child reaches for the flame and contacts it, the child learns the meaning of reaching for a flame. Seeing the flame is no longer simply a sensory perception, it is a meaningful perception (even if a young child cannot verbally explain that meaning). "It is no longer mere seeing; it is seeing-of-a-light-that-means-pain-when-contact-occurs" (Dewey, 1896: 360).

Stimuli take on meaning in terms of the consequences of our contact with or use of them (Mead, 1927a: 117-124, 131, 143f). Every time the child makes contact with or uses new objects, the child gains increased awareness of the properties of the objects in its physical world. "Through all this the child is busy getting the meaning of things. This is much the case in the play period of lower animals; they are learning things they will need later—meanings" (Mead, 1927a: 134).

LANGUAGE AND ROLE TAKING

In the previous two sections, we saw how children (and adults) attain an understanding of the meaning of social cues and objects without verbal mediation. As children acquire language,[50] they gain access to socially meaningful significant symbols that allow them to communicate ever more effectively with others and to carry on the inner conversation experienced as mind. As explained in Chapter 6, the inner conversation produces a heightened awareness of meaning and reflective consciousness. Naturally, children are not instantly capable of sophisticated levels of reflective consciousness, but after they begin talking most children tend to improve in reflective processes throughout the early years.

Children need to be involved actively in symbolic social interaction to learn the social meanings and ideas attached to significant symbols. "The process of getting an idea is, in the case of the infant, a process of intercourse with those about him, a social process. He can battle on by himself without getting any idea of what he is doing" (Mead, 1934: 107). Only through social interaction can children gain experience with the G-R-C triads on which the meaning of significant symbols is based. Because significant symbols are used in conventional manners, they are embedded in regular patterns of G-R-C triads, allowing the child to discover the meanings of these symbols (much as the infant had earlier discovered the meaning of the parents' nonvocal gestures). Because mother's words, "Mommy loves Janie," are typically enmeshed in G-R-C triads involving loving and caring interactions, Janie can discover their meaning from their usage. (As the word "love" appears in many other G-R-C triads involving caring events, the word will acquire a wider, more universal meaning [Mead, 1934: 82-90] than it would if it were only used in one particular G-R-C triad.) Because meaning is "objectively there" in the G-R-C triads present in symbolic social interaction (Mead, 1934: 76), children can discover those meanings and over the years gain increasing mastery of the significant symbols commonly used by their group.

When children first learn to talk, most become quite fascinated with language. Often "the child will converse for hours with himself, even constructing imaginary companions, who function in the child's growing self-consciousness as the processes of inner speech—of thought and imagination—function in the consciousness of the adult" (Mead, 1912/1964: 137). By conversing with imaginary companions, the child gains skills needed for carrying on the inner conversation of mind, which in turn produces a growing sense of consciousness, as significant symbols become increasingly meaningful to the child.

Not only do language and significant symbols permit the emergence of reflective consciousness and reflective intelligence, they allow the child to "take the rôle of the other" (Mead, 1913/1964: 146; 1917-18/1964: 214f; 1924-25/1964: 284; 1934: 73, 109, 138, 150f, 153, 161). The ability to take roles is of central importance in Mead's theory of socialization. Role taking consists of stepping out of one's own role and taking the social position of another person. It allows a person to view his or her own symbolic behavior from the perspective of the other, and partially understand the social roles of other people. Language and significant symbols are important mechanisms for role taking, though visual imagery, motor imagery, and nonverbal memories are also involved.[51]

Mead recognized that there are several different forms of role taking, ranging from the simplest forms seen in young children to the sophisticated forms that actors use when taking on theatrical roles (Mead, 1934: 161). Because the simpler forms of role taking can be done without the high level of self-consciousness that actors have, Mead stated that the phrase "taking the rôle of the other ... is a little unfortunate because it suggests an actor's attitude which is actually more sophisticated than that which is involved in our own experience. To this degree it does not correctly describe that which I have in mind" (Mead, 1934: 161). The remainder of this chapter describes various forms of role taking as they emerge in the socialization process, making it clear that most role taking is not done in the deliberate, self-conscious style used by actors.

Young children are capable of the simplest level of role taking as soon as they begin to use significant symbols (see Chapter 6). For example, when a little girl tells her mother, "I love you, Mommy," she hears her own words and comprehends their meanings much the same as the mother does. She understands that she has just said something caring to her mother. Hearing herself talk gives her an objective perception of her own behavior, as if she were standing outside of herself, "taking the rôle of the other," viewing herself from the role of another person. The use of vocal gestures in humans "involves not only communication in the sense in which birds and animals communicate with each other, but also an arousal in the individual himself of the response which he is calling out in the other individual, a taking of the rôle of the other, a tendency to act as the other person acts" (Mead, 1934: 73). It is almost as if the little girl were hearing her own words and meanings from the role of the mother, perhaps even sensing that the mother's response might be, "I love you, too, Janie."

This simplest level of role taking occurs in people of all ages, as a natural result of using significant symbols, even when people make no conscious effort to adopt the social role of another person. "We are unconsciously putting ourselves in the place of others and acting as others act." "We are, especially through the use of the vocal gestures, continually arousing in ourselves those responses which we call out in other persons, so that we are taking the attitudes of the other persons into our own conduct" (Mead, 1934: 69). Because we can "hear" the words of our inner conversation much the same as if they were spoken aloud, the mechanism of role taking operates just as well in the inner conversation as in overt social communication.

PLAY AND ROLE-PLAY

After children learn to use language, they begin types of play that are patterned on the social activities they see around them.[52] A little girl may play at being a mother; a little boy may play at being a policeman. In so doing, they are engaging in a second and more complex form of role taking.

Mead divided children's play into two types: role-play and games. Children develop simple forms of role-play before they learn to play games. The main difference between role-play and games is that games have rules, whereas role-play does not (Mead, 1924-25/1964: 285; 1927a: 145; 1934: 152). Both role-play and games involve role taking; however, the role taking in role-play is simpler than that in games, hence more easily mastered at an early age.

Mead dealt first with role-play, observing that much of children's early play is organized around social themes (Mead, 1934). "Play in this sense, especially the stage which precedes the organized games, is a play at something. A child plays at being a mother,[53] at being a teacher, at being a policeman; that is, it is taking different rôles..." (Mead, 1934: 150). Mead stressed that the child's play is different from the play of animals "in the sense that a child deliberately takes the rôle of another" (Mead, 1934: 150), whereas playing puppies or kittens do not. The child "may, of course, run away when he is chased, as a dog does, or he may turn around and strike back just as the dog does in his play. But that is not the same as playing at something. Children get together to 'play Indian'" (Mead, 1934: 150), which involves taking the role of Indians. Although role play is less structured than games with rules, it contains enough social structure to provide an easy starting point for the child in gaining knowledge about social roles and the structure of interactions.

Early childhood play can involve objects and nonverbal elements. For example, toys are frequently used in role-play, often having social importance even if not at a verbal level. "The child plays with all the things that the adult uses, although his objects may not be identical with the adult's, or they may be symbolic. A broken plate and a bit of wood will make a tea party for the child, whereas for us such a stimulus is inadequate" (Mead, 1927a: 134). By being symbolic of a whole plate, the broken plate serves the child quite well, helping the child to role-play an adult tea party and deal with the objects of the adult world at a symbolic level.

When the child alternates between playing two or more different roles in one scenario, the child learns various social roles and how to organize them in a socially meaningful manner. For example, the child may play "store" and take both of the major roles, as seller and buyer. "He plays that he is, for instance, offering himself something, and he buys it; and he gives a letter to himself and takes it away; he addresses himself as a parent, as a teacher; he arrests himself as a policeman" (Mead, 1934: 150-151). The words and actions of one role are stimuli that call up the other role.

> Here the very fact that he is ready to pay out money, for instance, arouses the attitude of the person who receives money; the very process is calling out in him the corresponding activities of the other person involved. The individual stimulates himself to the response which he is calling out in the other person, and then acts in some degree in response to that situation [Mead, 1934: 161]. . . . Such is the simplest form of being another to one's self. . . . The child says something in one character and responds in another character, and then his responding in another character is a stimulus to himself in the first character, and so the conversation goes on [Mead, 1934: 151].

By using words that adults use, children put themselves in the roles of adults. "If the individual does himself make use of something answering to the same gesture he observes, saying it over again to himself, putting himself in the rôle of the person who is speaking to him, then he has the meaning of what he hears, he has the idea: the meaning has become his" (Mead, 1934: 109). Thus, role-play with the words of adults helps children gain a partial understanding of the structure and meaning of adult social roles. "The child is acquiring the roles of those who belong to his society" (Mead, 1924-25/ 1964: 285). Note that the child is an active agent in his or her own socialization.

Role-play also influences the child's personality development. "Children play at being a parent, at being a teacher—vague personalities that are about them and which affect them and on which they depend. These are personalities which they take, rôles they play, and in so far control the development of their own personality" (Mead, 1934: 153). If a little girl likes her kindergarten teacher and frequently role-plays being such a teacher, she may acquire some of the interests and characteristics of her teacher. Through playing many different roles, the child gradually acquires her own unique combination of personality traits—and a sense of self. Inasmuch as these internal qualities emerge from using external role models such as mother, father, policemen, and teachers, we can understand Mead's rationale for studying socialization from the outside to the inside (Mead, 1914: 53, 55f, 62, 68; 1927a: 156; 1934: 7-8): First, he examined language, social processes, and role taking; then he showed how these external variables give rise to inner qualities such as the inner conversation, personality, and a sense of self.

The child's ability to evaluate and control his or her own behavior arises, in part, from taking the role of the parents. Thoughts of carrying out a certain action call up "memory images of the responses of those about us, the memory images of those responses of others which were in answer to like actions. Thus the child can think about his conduct as good or bad only as he reacts to his own acts in the remembered words of his parents" (Mead, 1913/1964: 146). Role taking makes us conscious of self and lifts instincts "out of the level of the mechanical response to biologically determined stimuli and brings them within the sweep of self-conscious direction inside of the larger group activity" (Mead, 1917-18/1964: 215).

The young child's role taking is much simpler than the role taking seen in adults when they consciously try to imagine themselves being in the place of another. The young child does not have as clear a concept of self as the adults have, hence does not clearly discriminate the differences between other people's roles and his or her own roles. When role taking, the young child, "before his own ego is definitely formed, ... does not make the distinction between himself and others which the adult makes. The child's self is for the time being in the others. He has not isolated and organized the ego as the adults have" (Mead, 1914: 66). When playing mother and using mother's words, the little girl is taking over mother's words and meanings, and in her own mind becoming mother. Thus, the child is more strongly influenced by the roles of others than are adults, who can clearly distinguish that adopted roles are not the same as their own roles. Only as the child develops a clearer concept of his or her own "self"—with unique roles and personality traits—will the child be able to do role taking in a more abstract and detached manner.

Naturally, neither children nor adults can take the role of another person as that other person knows it. "When one is taking the part of another, the scheme which takes place in our own manner of speaking is his manner as we know it" (Mead, 1914: 70). What we know of other people is based on their external words and actions, rather than on direct observations of their inner thoughts and feelings (Mead, 1914: 62): "If you carry on a discussion with another person in your mind, you use the way you have heard him speak" (Mead, 1914: 70). "The manner by which an individual takes the role of another is not by merging his personality in the other but by speaking of one individual in place of the other" (Mead, 1914: 69). Thus, role taking does not guarantee that one person can accurately adopt a perfect copy of the second person's role, especially as the second person subjectively experiences that role. Therefore, much of role taking is filled in by imagination (Mead, 1914: 66f)—though, of course, there is no easy way to know when our imagined information is right or wrong.

GAMES

Role-play is structured to some degree—for instance, by the constraints of adopting the role of a teacher or a policeman. Games are more strictly organized than is role-play, as the child must play within the structure imposed by rules. "This organization is put in the form of the rules of the game. Children take a great interest in rules" (Mead, 1934: 152). Part of the interest and challenge of games is in staying within the rules. A child can hop from one side of the sidewalk to the other, pretending to be a mountain climber hopping from rock to rock; but in the game of hopscotch, the child is challenged by having to hop skillfully from one space to another, according to the rules of the game. Winning at games depends on learning rules and playing skillfully within the framework of the rules. While playing games, children learn how to organize and control their own actions according to rules.

Naturally, there are times when the rules of a game do not work to a child's advantage. In a baseball game, one team may be losing because the second team is good at earning bases by bunting. The first team may create a new rule—"No bunties"—and perhaps threaten to stop playing if the new rule is not accepted. Children "make rules on the spot in order to help themselves out of difficulties. Part of the enjoyment of the game is to get these rules" (Mead, 1934: 152). Thus, children learn not only to follow rules, but to create and manipulate them.

The rule-organized structure of games requires a more sophisticated form of role taking than is seen in role-play. A baseball team works together best if each player knows how *all* the other players will respond at any given moment. If each player can role take with all the others, the team can coordinate and act as a unit. "If we contrast play with the situation in an organized game, we note the essential difference that the child who plays in a game must be ready to take the attitude of everyone else involved in that game, and that these different rôles must have a definite relationship to each other" (Mead, 1934: 151). If there is a chance for a double play, each player must know how the others will contribute to making it.

> He must know what everyone else is going to do in order to carry out his own play. He has to take all of these roles. They do not all have to be present in consciousness at the same time, but at some moments he has to have three or four individuals present in his own attitude, such as the one who is going to throw the ball, the one who is going to catch it, and so on [Mead, 1934: 151].

Of course, it takes years before children master the advanced levels of role taking needed for truly sophisticated game play.

Games with teams facilitate the emergence of the generalized other in the child's consciousness.

> Each one of [a team player's] own acts is determined by his assumption of the action of the others who are playing the game. What he does is controlled by his being everyone else on that team, at least in so far as those attitudes affect his own particular response. We get then an "other" which is an organization of the attitudes of those involved in the same process [Mead, 1934: 154].

This "other" person that reflects the "organized community" or the whole team "may be called 'the generalized other.' The attitude of the generalized other is the attitude of the whole community" (Mead, 1934: 154). When the shortstop has a good understanding of the whole team's response to a chance for a double play, the shortstop can think of the whole team in terms of the "generalized other" and synchronize with all the other players to produce an organized, unified team response.

Games help the child learn to synchronize with the organic whole of team actions. "It is not sufficient for him merely to take the attitudes of other human individuals toward himself and toward one another ... he must also ... take their attitudes toward the various phases or aspects of the common social activity ... in which, as members of an organized society or social group, they are all engaged..." (Mead, 1934: 154-155). This requires that the person must develop a generalized approach to the attitudes and organized actions of the whole group. He needs to "take the general attitudes of all other such individuals with reference to these processes ... and to the organized social whole ... and ... direct his own behavior accordingly" (Mead, 1934: 155).

In role-play, the child takes one role at a time; but in games, the child must role take with the whole team, respond to the generalized other, and integrate with the whole organic social process (Mead, 1927a: 145; 1934: 158ff).[54] Games give children valuable training in coordinating with larger groups and prepare them for adopting adult roles synchronized with the organized whole of society.

Team games help children learn the self-control needed for coordinating in group activities. If the team is to function as a unit, all the players must allow their actions to be at least partially controlled by the needs, rules, and social responses of the whole group. "It is in the form of the generalized other that the social process influences the behavior of the individuals involved in it and carrying in on..." (Mead, 1934: 155). To the degree that people learn to be good team players, they learn to organize their actions in response to the generalized other—the actions of the whole group. In this manner, "the community exercises control over the conduct of its individual members; for it is in this form that the social process or community enters as a determining factor into the individual's thinking" (Mead, 1934: 155).

As the individual develops facility in thinking in terms of the generalized other, the generalized other—that is, the community— plays an increasingly important role in structuring the individual's private world of thought. "Our thinking is an inner conversation in which we may be taking the roles of specific acquaintances over against ourselves, but usually it is with what I have termed the 'generalized other' that we converse, and so obtain to the levels of abstract thinking, and that impersonality, that so-called objectivity that we cherish" (Mead, 1924-25/1964: 288). Because the generalized other is an abstract "other" that reflects the organized views of the whole social system, it blends the perspectives of all individuals in terms of the integrated whole, hence tends to be more objective than is the view of any single individual if taken in isolation from the group. For the child, learning to think in terms of the generalized other marks an important transition to a more objective form of self-consciousness. "The game represents the passage in the life of the child from taking the rôle of others in play to the organized part that is essential to self-consciousness in the full sense of the term" (Mead, 1934: 152).

When baseball players learn to think in terms of the generalized other, they acquire a common perspective on all facets of the game (Mead, 1927b/1964: 313). If they all think in terms of the generalized other, each will find the same meanings as the others in all the stimuli relevant to the game, which helps assure that all relevant significant symbols call up the same meanings in the different players (Mead, 1922/1964: 244ff). As children move beyond games and learn to re-spond to the generalized other of larger society, this more universal generalized other helps them learn to find the same meanings as other social members in an ever larger number of significant symbols. For society to function, significant symbols (such as the words "private property") must call up the same general meanings in all members, "so that when one says such a thing he calls out in himself the response of the others. He is calling out the response of what I have called a generalized other. That which makes society possible is such common reponses..." (Mead, 1934: 161). Thus as children learn to think in terms of the generalized other, they gain increased ability to understand their social world as others do and to synchronize with the larger society into which they are moving.

ROLE TAKING AFTER CHILDHOOD

Language, role-play, and games introduce children to role taking. As people make the transition into adulthood, their role taking often changes and develops further. Mead described some of the adult variations in role taking. First, after childhood role taking tends to become increasingly abstract. The child's role-play is often like a drama, involving vivid fantasy images of the imaginary people or ac-tors, the dramatis personae on a mental stage.

Later the inner stage changes into the forum and workshop of thought.
The features and intonations of the dramatis personae fade out and the

emphasis falls upon the meaning of the inner speech, the imagery becomes merely the barely necessary cues. But the mechanism remains social, and at any moment the process may become personal [Mead, 1913/1964: 147].

Thus, adults still have access to highly personalized role taking based on vivid images of specific individuals; but adults tend to focus more on the words and meanings than on the personal qualities of the speakers in their inner conversation.

In addition, as the inner conversation increasingly involves the generalized other, it gradually ceases to be an inner conversation with specific individuals and becomes increasingly abstract. This is especially true because as the child moves beyond games the generalized other is based increasingly on the structure of social institutions, rather than the rules of childhood games (Mead, 1934: 162, 167, 194). Thus, the generalized other becomes ever more a faceless abstraction that represents the general response of the whole community. An inner conversation with the generalized other helps us see beyond the perspectives of single individuals and grasp more universal meanings of the whole social process. Thus, it often provides a more rational and objective (Mead, 1924-25/1964: 288; 1927a: 147, 150f, 163; 1934: 167f, 191, 334) analysis than is available to children in their fantasy dialogues with imaginary companions.

Second, to some degree we all learn to become actors. The photographer tells the child to put on a happy face. The teenager practices various lines and styles that he hopes will impress his date. The college graduate learns to put on a facade of sophistication when going for a job interview. Although few of us gain the skills of professional actors, to the degree that we gain these skills, we develop a type of role taking that differs from the simplest forms of role taking that are based on hearing significant symbols as if from the role of another person (Mead, 1934: 161).

Third, after years of social experience, people often gain increased ability to understand the feelings and emotions of others through empathy and sympathy. Mead often referred to sympathy, which is a combination of caring for another and empathetic role taking with that person (Mead, 1914: 47, 62, 67, 71, 91, 93; 1930/1964: 397ff; 1934: 298ff, 366, 376). Sympathy for a person consists of "standing in his own shoes and speaking with his intonation" (Mead, 1914: 67); it means "putting yourself in his place" (Mead, 1934: 366). "We tend to reserve the term 'sympathetic,' however, for those kindly acts and attitudes which are the essential binding-cords in the life of any human group" (Mead, 1934: 366). Sympathy helps us have thoughts and feelings that are similar to those of the other person.

We speak of this interest on the emotional side as "sympathy"—passing into the attitude of the other, taking the rôle of the other, feeling the other's joys and sorrows. That is the affective side of it. What we call the "intellectual side," the "rational side," is the recognition of common stimuli, of common emotions which call out responses in every member of the group [Mead, 1936: 375].

In this context, Mead stated that even sympathetic role taking is never completely accurate. "The other is a different person and, being different, his suffering is different from mine, but he is a suffering being to whom I react immediately. Other individuals exist for us as having inner ideas, which in a certain sense we can never penetrate" (Mead, 1914: 62). Inasmuch as each individual is unique, no one can have a complete understanding of the thoughts and feelings of others.

Fourth, economic processes of buying and selling require role taking (Mead, 1924-25/1964: 282-284; 1934: 289-302). In order for the marketplace to work, both the buyer and seller must put themselves in the position of the other in order to see how much the other wants the item that is for sale.[55]

If you are going to carry on the economic process successfully, you have to come into closer and closer relationship with the other individual, identify yourself not simply in the particular matter of exchange, but find out what he wants and why he wants it, what will be the conditions of payment, the particular character of the goods desired, and so on. You have to identify yourself with him more and more [Mead, 1934: 298]. ... One cannot exchange otherwise than by putting one's self in the attitude of the other party to the bargain [Mead, 1924-25/1964: 283].

Although Mead saw the economic process as generally a valuable source of social integration (Mead, 1934: 292ff), he was aware that economic motivations can lead people to use role taking to take advantage of others.

We are rather scornful of the attitude of salesmanship which modern business emphasizes—salesmanship which seems always to carry with it hypocrisy, to advocate putting one's self in the attitude of the other so as to trick him into buying something he does not want. Even if we do not regard this as justifiable, we can at least recognize that even here there is the assumption that the individual has to take the attitude of the other, that the recognition of the interest of the other is essential to a successful trade [Mead, 1934: 298].

Fifth, people tend to think of and take the roles of animals and physical objects as if they were social beings (Mead, 1932: 122, 136, 138; 1934: 182-186; 1938: 154, 475). "We talk to nature; we address the clouds, the sea, the tree, and objects about us" (Mead, 1934: 184).

There are two ways to take the role of nature: with either a magical or a scientific point of view. Children and "primitive" peoples often relate to nature in a magical manner—"Rain, rain, go away; come again another day"—as if talking and coaxing could change natural events, the way talk can change other people's actions. On a cloudy day, a person may wish the sun would come out: "Come on, sun, you can break through." The person is taking the role of the elements, feeling that with a little encouragement the sun certainly could break through, and then offering that social support. "These are attitudes which perhaps we normally cover up, but which are revealed to us in numerous situations" (Mead, 1934: 186).

By adulthood, many people shift from the magical point of view to a more scientific perspective. The scientist also takes the role of nature, but in a more critical manner (Mead, 1934: 186). "An engineer who is constructing a bridge is talking to nature..." (Mead, 1934: 185). The engineer uses data and empirically derived equations to imagine how the bridge will respond to various loads and high winds. "In his thinking he is taking the attitude of physical things" (Mead, 1934: 185). If calculations show that the original design is too weak, the engineer may feel terrible while imagining the bridge collapsing in a high wind. The scientific view is different from magic because it is based on data about nature rather than the "assumption that physical things ... think and act as we do" (Mead, 1934: 186).

Sixth, although children role take mostly with parents and other members of their micro social environment, adults often learn to role take with people on a much broader scale. Mead was concerned with resolving social conflict and injustice, ending war, and building a better world (Mead, 1899; 1914: 97-105; 1915; 1917-18; 1924-25; 1929c; 1930; 1934: 303-328); and he believed that one method[56] for attaining these goals was to help people learn to take the role of other people from all nations and walks of life. The more successfully that individuals can view social problems from numerous perspectives, the more likely they are to understand all points of view when seeking solutions to social problems.

Unfortunately, many social institutions, complex organizations, and distant people are very abstract. It is difficult to role take with social structures or people who are mere abstractions, such as multinational corporations or the poor of the Third World. How can we overcome abstraction? "Our need for imagery is fundamental, for it is by that means we can put ourselves in other people's places" (Mead, 1914: 97). "The ideal of human society cannot exist as long as it is impossible for individuals to enter into the attitudes of those whom they are affecting in the performance of their own peculiar functions"

(Mead, 1934: 328). We need concrete information about people if we are to imagine what it is like to live their lives and feel their problems.

Mead suggested methods for helping people relate to others in concrete terms so they can role take with real people rather than abstractions (Mead, 1914: 97-101). Newspapers, photographs, radio, movies, short stories, plays, literature, and art—especially in the style of realism[57]—can help us understand others in concrete terms, so we can put ourselves in the place of others, take their perspective on social problems, and seek the most sensitive solutions. "The social function of the artist is to provide imagery for thinking from all points of view. The community cannot bring itself to realize these other relations until it gets imagery from the artist" (Mead, 1914: 100). "Making abstract relations concrete constitutes social advance" (Mead, 1914: 80).

Although some people naturally seek an ever broader understanding of the human condition, others need input from artists, mass media, political activists, and so forth to broaden their social perspectives. "The labor movement has forced communities to think in social terms instead of abstract terms. People have been forced either from the outside or from the inside to put themselves into other people's places" (Mead, 1914: 98).

* * *

Mead saw role taking as an important means of socialization, bringing people together and increasing understanding. Not everyone becomes highly proficient in role taking; but Mead believed that developing our capacity for role taking would help in creating a better world (Mead, 1914: 91-102; 1917-18; 1924-25; 1930).

8

The Self and Society

Mead wrote extensively on the self and the reciprocal interactions of the self and society. In one sense, a person's self consists of the person's thoughts about the unified whole of his or her own body, thoughts, emotions, personality, and actions. Thus, it is a part of the person's private world of thoughts (h in Figure 1; see Chapter 1). However, as Mead repeatedly emphasized (Mead, 1927a: 148-163; 1910a; 1912; 1913; 1924-25; 1934: 140, 149, 186f, 191, 200ff, 222ff), the self is inherently social in nature; thus it must be considered as part of the whole social process. "The self is a social entity that cannot be located, as the Greeks located the psyche, in the heart, head, or organs. It is a social entity that must be related to the entire body, and only insofar as the self is related to the body is it related to the environment" (Mead, 1927a: 148). Thus, "the self involves a unity" of body, behavior, and environment (a, b, c, d, and h in Figure 1); and it is not to be conceived dualistically, as something separate from social processes (Mead, 1927a: 148).

The self can come into existence only in terms of society and interaction with other selves (Mead, 1910a; 1912; 1913; 1927a: 153f; 1934: 149-164, 172, 186); therefore it owes its existence to the micro and macro social environment (b and c in Figure 1). All through life, a person's self develops through social interaction and is influenced by micro and macro social processes (arrows e and f in Figure 1). As a person develops an ever better organized self, that self has increasing impact on micro and macro social processes (arrows i and j in Figure 1). Although some people change society more than others, all people affect society to at least some degree (Mead, 1934: 200, 215f). There is a continuous, dynamic interplay between self and society in which both self and society influence and change each other (Mead, 1908/1964: 88; 1922/1964: 240; 1923/1964: 266; 1934: 129, 199-203, 214-217, 308-310).

This chapter traces the origin of the self, showing how the self takes its structure from the structure of society and why each individual—with a unique self—can make valuable contributions to his or her society.

NONDUALISM

There is no mind-body dualism implied in Mead's view of the self: "The self involves a unity; it is there in the social process. . . . It is the center about which the individual is organized, and the body is an integral part of the self." "We are thus tied to the body insofar as we have a self" (Mead, 1927a: 148). "That self is not made up from psychical stuff" (Mead, 1927a: 107).

Descartes and other dualists had conceived of the self as a type of psychical substance that had no functional relationship to the physical and social environment; but Mead viewed the self as a natural part of the human social world, a phase of social processes. "The self is not so much a substance as a process in which the conversation of gestures has been internalized within an organic form. This process does not exist for itself, but is simply a phase of the whole social organization of which the individual is a part" (Mead, 1934: 178). This position reflects Mead's nondualist view that mind and self emerge from and are an organic part of social processes.

Although Descartes's first principle—"I think, therefore I am"—assumed the primacy of the self and subjective experiences, Mead argued that social processes are necessary preconditions for the emergence of self. "What I want particularly to emphasize is the temporal and logical pre-existence of the social process to the self-conscious individual that arises in it" (Mead, 1934: 186). "[W]e do not assume that there is a self to begin with. Self is not presupposed as a stuff out of which the world arises. Rather the self arises in the world" (Mead, 1927a: 107). "Other selves in a social environment logically antedate the consciousness of self which introspection analyzes" (Mead, 1910a/1964: 111). Although introspective, dualistic logic leads to the view that "each self is an island," isolated from all others (Mead, 1910a/1964: 107), Mead saw the self as inherently social: "The process out of which the self arises is a social process which implies interaction of individuals in the group, implies the pre-existence of the group" (Mead, 1934: 164). Even though a person's self is a highly personal thing that only that person can possess and intimately experience, it is a gift to the individual from society and always remains part of the social process.

EMERGENCE OF SELF

Mead provided both evolutionary and developmental perspectives on the emergence of the self. First, "lower animals do not have selves" (Mead, 1927a: 107). "Selves have appeared late in vertebrate evolution." "[T]he self that is central to all so-called mental experience has appeared only in the social conduct of human vertebrates" (Mead, 1924-25/1964: 283). Selves could only emerge after humans evolved to the point of using significant symbols: Significant symbols allow a person to take the role of the listener and thereby get the objective, outsider's view of his or her own self as a social object. "Only within the social process at its higher levels, only in terms of the more developed forms of the social environment or social situation, does the total individual organism become an object to itself, and hence self-conscious..." (Mead, 1934: 172).

Second, the self arises only slowly in childhood through symbolic social interaction. "The self is not present in the early months of life" (Mead, 1927a: 107). "The self is something which has a development; it is not initially there, at birth, but arises in the process of social experience and activity, that is, develops in the given individual as a result of his relations to that process as a whole and to other individuals within that process" (Mead, 1934: 135).

"In infancy we can see the beginnings of the self arising" (Mead, 1927a: 144). It takes years for the self to emerge, as the infant gradually acquires an objective view of his or her own body and behavior. "Self arises in conduct, when the individual becomes a social object in experience to himself." "It is a development that arises gradually in the life of the infant and presumably arose gradually in the life of the race" (Mead, 1922/1964: 243).

In early infancy, the baby sees his or her own arms and legs moving, and these stimuli appear much as other stimuli in the environment—interesting external things to watch, but not integrated parts of the self. "Until the rise of his self-consciousness in the process of social experience, the individual experiences his body—its feelings and sensations—merely as an immediate part of his environment, not as his own, not in terms of self-consciousness" (Mead, 1934: 172). Only after extended experience does the child begin to piece together perceptions of the stimuli from different body parts in a unified conception of self. "It will be some time before he can successfully unite the different parts of his own body, such as his hands and feet, which he sees and feels, into a single object" (Mead, 1912/1964: 138). Even after the infant relates body parts to the whole body, it is a long time before a fully integrated conception of self emerges. "In the organization of the baby's physical experience the appearance of his body as a unitary thing ... will be relatively late..." (Mead, 1912/1964: 138).

Understanding how *other* people relate to themselves as selves is essential for children to realize that they also have selves. "The form of the social object must be found first of all in the experience of other selves" (Mead, 1912/1964: 138). "The child's early social percepts are of others. After these, arise incomplete and partial selves—or 'me's'— which are quite analogous to the child's percepts of the hands and feet, which precede his perception of himself as a whole" (Mead, 1912/ 1964: 139). However, the unified perception of self does not appear "until the child is able to experience himself as he experiences other selves," namely by perceiving his whole self from an external, objective point of view through role taking (Mead, 1912/1964: 139).

This is a clear example of Mead's view that internal psychological events are organized from the outside to the inside (Mead, 1914: 53, 55f, 62f, 68, 74; 1927a: 156; 1934: 7-8). "We have a social consciousness which is organized from the periphery toward the center" (Mead, 1914: 55). In numerous places Mead stated that children develop a sense of self only after they understand other individuals as personalities and selves (Mead, 1910a; 1912/1964: 138f; 1914: 53-56, 62f; 1927a: 107, 156; 1934: 135-164). "Social consciousness is organized from the outside in. The social percepts which first arise are those of other selves." "It is only after he has reached the point of communicating with himself that his own self-consciousness can arise" (Mead, 1914: 53). "You cannot have consciousness of self without consciousness of other selves." "The 'alteri' [others] arise earlier than the self, both in the child and the race" (Mead, 1914: 63).

Role Taking. For children to obtain a clear view of themselves as selves, they need to take the role of others so they can view themselves as social objects, as others do. Mead described several stages in the development of self through role taking in childhood: (1) early use of significant symbols, (2) play, and (3) games (Mead, 1924-25/1964: 284; 1934: 144-146).

First, for self to emerge there has to be a means by which "the individual should thus take an objective, impersonal attitude toward himself, that he should become an object to himself" (Mead, 1934: 138). When children begin to use language, they gain access to the simplest form of role taking, in which they hear their own significant symbols in an objective manner and get an objective view of their own thoughts and utterances. It is via the use of significant symbols and role taking "that we have behavior in which the individuals become objects to themselves" (Mead, 1934: 139). "The self can exist for the individual only if he assumes the roles of the others." "We appear as selves in our conduct insofar as we ourselves take the attitude that others take toward us..." (Mead, 1924-25/1964: 284). As children gain increasing capacity for role taking, they develop increasingly complex and integrated conceptions of self.

Because self only arises through language and role taking, it is inherently social in nature. "Only by social means—only by taking the attitudes of others toward himself—is [a person] able to become an object to himself" (Mead, 1934: 226). "Self-consciousness involves the individual's becoming an object to himself by taking the attitudes of other individuals toward himself within an organized setting of social relationships, and that unless the individual had thus become an object to himself he would not be self-conscious or have a self at all" (Mead, 1934: 225).

Second, after children begin role-play, they further develop their personality and selves. When children play the roles of others, they use parts of those roles "in building a self" (Mead, 1934: 150). While playing house, children take the roles of mother and father, thereby acquiring aspects of their parents' interests and selves. "It is only as the child does this that he comes to have a full self" (Mead, 1927a: 145). The roles that children play (e.g., parent, teacher, policeman) "control the development of their own personality" (Mead, 1934: 153).

The self is modeled on others. "The child fashions his own self on the model of other selves." "The child's consciousness of its own self is quite largely the reflection of the attitudes of others toward him" Mead, 1914: 54). The perception of the parents comes first; and that perception influences the child's view of self. "At first, the child accepts the judgment of others about himself; not all ideas that go to build up an organized self are brought together till after the self of the parent is organized" (Mead, 1914: 62).

Third, games facilitate the further development of an integrated, unified personality. Before reaching the game phase of socialization, the child "is not organized into a whole. The child has no definite character, no definite personality" (Mead, 1934: 159). However, as children begin playing games, they learn to synchronize with larger groups and organize their own responses in relation to the rules of the game and the actions of the whole group. "The game, in other words, requires a whole self, whereas play requires only pieces of the self" (Mead, 1927a: 145). In role-play, a child may focus on only a fragment of the role that is being played out, without understanding the whole role; but games demand a more organized self if the child is to coordinate with others. Games, with their rules and structure, help the child develop a more organized self. "The game has a logic, so that such an organization of the self is rendered possible..." (Mead, 1934:

158-159). As the child plays games, "he is becoming an organic member of society" (Mead, 1934: 159).

Because games help the child think in terms of the generalized other, the child can increasingly "see himself as the whole group sees him," which helps the child acquire a "unity of personality" (Mead, 1922/1964: 245-246). "And it is this generalized other in his experience which provides him with a self" (Mead, 1924-25/1964: 285). "When the child can take the attitude of the entire group, he can come back to himself the same way and thus come to have self-consciousness and a unitary self" (Mead, 1927a: 147).

Games provide an important transition to adulthood in large, complex societies. Although modern societies are structurally too complex for the young child to comprehend or interact with, the child can relate to the structure of games. "The importance of the game is that it lies entirely inside the child's own experience..." (Mead, 1934: 159). Through game play, the child learns to cope with structured social situations: "He becomes a something which can function in the organized whole, and thus tends to determine himself in his relationship with the group to which he belongs." "Such is the process by which a personality arises" (Mead, 1934: 160). The rules and structure of games help the child organize various pieces of the self into a whole personality. "The game is then an illustration of the situation out of which an organized personality arises" (Mead, 1934: 159). Other illustrations are found as the child gradually enters the adult world, with its complex rules and structures; and "real-life" social experiences begin to replace games as important socializing situations.

After the child can relate to the generalized other of games, the child gradually learns to conceive of the generalized other in terms of broader social institutions (Mead, 1934: 162, 167, 194). Namely, the generalized other comes to represent increasingly abstract social relations. Through role taking with a generalized other based on the structure of the whole society, the individual gains an ever broader and more abstract perspective on self, and this higher level of understanding helps to further develop and organize the individual's personality and self. "A person is a personality because he belongs to a community, because he takes over the institutions of that community into his own conduct." "Such, in a certain sense, is the structure of a man's personality" (Mead, 1934: 162). Of course, even in "highly developed, organized and complicated" societies, our personalities and selves are not patterned exclusively on abstract, institutional structures: Even in adulthood, the self continues to be influenced by concrete, personal relations with other individuals (Mead, 1934: 157f).

STRUCTURE

Because the self is structured from the outside to the inside, it reflects the structure of role models, games, rules, generalized others, and institutions in the individual's social world. This structural theme was central to Mead's theory of self. "The individual possesses a self only in relation to the selves of other members of his social group; and the structure of his self expresses or reflects the general behavior pattern of this social group to which he belongs, just as does the structure of the self of every other individual belonging to this social group" (Mead, 1934: 164; also see Mead, 1934: 222). In fact, the structure of the whole mind reflects the structure of society.[58] A person's thoughts reflect the workings of a "mind whose inner structure he has taken from the community to which he belongs" (Mead, 1934: 270; also see Mead, 1932: 87; 1934: 155).

Each individual's socialization structures the mind and self in two important and complementary ways, producing (1) common traits that are shared with others, and (2) unique, personal traits that make the person a distinctive individual (Mead, 1929c; 1934: 163, 317-328). As a result, each person feels a sense of belonging *and* a sense of being different from others. "There lie in all of us both of these attitudes" (Mead, 1929c/1964: 357). The balance of these two can vary considerably from person to person: Some feel a strong sense of belonging and others do not; some feel like they have special unique viewpoints on life and others do not.

The common, shared qualities are needed for society to function smoothly. For one self to understand and coordinate with other selves, these selves must share a certain amount of common structure. It is the generalized other and institutions that help socialize people in different parts of society to have the same responses, shared interests, and common organization of selves needed for understanding and synchronizing with others. The shared qualities are the

> structures upon which the self is constructed, the framework of the self, as it were. Of course we are not only what is common to all: each one of the selves is different from everyone else; but there has to be such a common structure ... in order that we may be members of a community at all. We cannot be ourselves unless we are also members in whom there is a community of attitudes which control the attitudes of all [Mead, 1934: 163-164]. ... It is only in our common interests and our identities with others that there is found the stuff out of which social selves are made... [Mead, 1929c/1964: 357].

The same socialization process that fosters similarities among individuals also generates differences. "The common social origin and constitution of individual selves and their structures does not preclude wide individual differences and variations among them..." (Mead, 1934: 201). Because no two people have exactly the same roles or locations in the social structure, they have different socializations and develop different selves. "Every individual self has its own peculiar individuality, its own unique pattern [which reflects the whole, but] does so from its own particular and unique standpoint within that process..." (Mead, 1934: 201). "Each one of us has an outlook on the universe which belongs to each one of us alone, and it appears insofar as we have in us a reflective consciousness in which life seems to be interpreted" (Mead, 1936: 411; see also Mead, 1924-25/1964: 276).

People like to know how they are different from others. "We want to recognize ourselves in our differences from other persons" (Mead, 1934: 205). We do this by self-observation and comparison with others. "Since it is a social self, it is a self that is realized in its relationship to others" (Mead, 1934: 204). According to Mead, part of feeling unique comes from locating ways in which we are different from and "superior" to others. The differences can be large or small; but they are of great importance in giving the individual a sense of uniqueness. "It is a means for the preservation of the self. We have to distinguish ourselves from other people and this is accomplished by doing something which other people cannot do, or cannot do as well" (Mead, 1934: 208). Most people restrain themselves in emphasizing their own strengths and areas of superiority. "We are careful, of course, not directly to plume ourselves. It would seem childish to intimate that we take satisfaction in showing that we can do something better than others. We take a great deal of pains to cover up such a situation; but actually we are vastly gratified" (Mead, 1934: 205).

Multiple Selves. Mead's discussion of multiple selves reflects his structural view of the self. Taking the role of the generalized other and the larger community, people tend to perceive themselves as unified beings. "Normally, within the sort of community as a whole to which we belong, there is a unified self, but that may be broken up" (Mead, 1934: 143). The breaking of the self into several parts is especially likely when we interact with different people who place different demands on us. "We often recognize the lines of cleavage that run through us." "What we have here is a situation in which there can be different selves, and it is dependent upon the set of social reactions that is involved as to which self we are going to be" (Mead, 1934: 143).

When we change from one set of social roles to another, different parts of our selves are emphasized.

We carry on a whole series of different relationships to different people. We are one thing to one man and another thing to another.... We divide ourselves up in all sorts of different selves with reference to our acquaintances. We discuss politics with one and religion with another. There are all sorts of different selves answering to all sorts of different social reactions [Mead, 1934: 142].

It is because we can put ourselves into the roles of others and see their different points of view, that we can be different things for different people. "It is the possibility of putting ourselves in other's places that accounts for these different selves. We carry models indicating what we ought to be in different circumstances" (Mead, 1914: 70). Because we can be different people to different audiences, "a multiple personality is in a certain sense normal. . ." (Mead, 1934: 142).[59]

For most of us, the multiple selves are integrated into a larger, unified whole. "We are all persons of multiple selves, but all of these have their relation to the organic fundamental self" (Mead, 1914: 71). The unity of the self is derived from the unity of larger social processes, if our self is intermeshed with other individuals, teams, or institutions that are organized in a meaningful manner. "The unity that makes up the self is the unity of a social organization that makes one feel part of the social process.... The unity of the self involves an organization of all the other selves" (Mead, 1927a: 164).

The Emergence of an Increasingly Structured Self. The self of the child is not as fully developed and structured as the self of adults; and there is variation in the level of organization of the self among adults. The emergence of a highly developed and structured self is influenced by several factors.

First, the complexity of the self depends in part on a person's ability to take the role of others and view the self from the perspective of others (Mead, 1913; 1914: 70ff, 95; 1927a: 164; 1934: 171, 194). Some people are relatively unreflective, with limited capacity for role taking, which limits their self-awareness. "An unsophisticated person is relatively unconscious of self" (Mead, 1914: 72). The more reflective person is likely to gain increasing self-awareness with age and experience, thereby reaching an ever-better organized conception of self.

Second, problematic situations provide important experiences for the development of the self (Mead, 1913; 1914: 74f). Conflicts and problems cause us to stop and reflect on the possible solutions to the problems, which may necessitate establishing new relationships between our self and others, society, or the environment. At each phase of development, the self is organized for dealing with common events. When new problems arise, "there is some disintegration in this organization, and different tendencies appear in reflective thought as different voices in conflict with each other. In a sense the old self has disintegrated, and out of the moral process a new self arises" (Mead,

1913/1964: 147). The moral process consists of evaluating the new situation in terms of the multiple values of the self and society. As we draw on social values and information in solving problems, "enlarged and more adequate personalities may emerge" (Mead, 1913/1964: 148). As a new self arises, "the whole self is reconstructed in its relation to the other selves whose relations are essential to its personality. The growth of the self arises out of a partial disintegration [of the old self] ... and the consequent appearance of the new self" (Mead, 1913/1964: 149).

Third, the structural complexity and integration of a person's society influence the level of development of the self. "The consciousness of the individual in a sense is a reflection of the complex social situation in which he lives." "He imports into himself these [social] relations. When we get a social consciousness which answers to these complex relations, we have a higher mentality" (Mead, 1914: 81). In small, simple, early societies, role taking with all other members of the society and understanding the social organization was easier than in large, complex, modern societies; but the person was limited to concrete relations with a small number of people. "The average individual in a village (in the past) never got beyond that except by certain abstract relations, but now we can deal in very concrete fashion with a vast number of persons. We can become cosmopolitan" (Mead, 1914: 79). Through travel, art, literature, and the news media, we can become aware of a large range of the human condition, and role taking with the larger whole of a complex society helps us develop selves with increasingly complex and sophisticated structures. Though many people do not role take with the larger range of modern society, Mead clearly saw that this was a beneficial process (Mead, 1914: 93-105). "This getting of the broad activities of any given social whole ... within the experiential field of any one of the individuals involved ... in that whole is ... the essential basis and prerequisite of the fullest development of that individual's self" (Mead, 1934: 155).

THE "I" AND THE "ME"[60]

Mead divided the self into two distinctive parts: the "I" and the "me."[61] The "I" is the subject; the "me" is the object. The "I" is the self that acts; the "me" is the self that we see as an object when we observe our self from the role of the other. When we talk with someone, it is the "I" who does the talking. As soon as we hear our own words, we have responded to our self as an object of observation, hence as a "me." Thus, consciousness of the "me" arises through role taking: "This takes place through the ability to put ourselves in the place of others, a process in which one builds up the 'me' that one knows" (Mead, 1914: 94). The "me" is a composite view of the self as seen from the perspectives of the people we know and the generalized other. "The individual sees himself from the point of view of other individuals and they form the point of view of himself" (Mead, 1914: 95).

We can never observe the part of our self called the "I." Any attempt to observe the "I" only reveals a "me"—that is, the self we see through self-observation. Therefore, it follows that "the self cannot appear in consciousness as an 'I,' that it is always an object, i.e., a 'me'..." (Mead, 1913/1964: 142). Only the "me" can be brought directly into awareness. "The 'I' lies beyond the range of immediate experience" (Mead, 1912/1964: 140).

In essence, the self of the present instant is the "I." As soon as the "I" acts, the act slips into the past where we can observe it in our memory of the previous moment as a part of the "me." "The simplest way of handling the problem would be in terms of memory." "The 'I' of this moment is present in the 'me' of the next moment." "I become a 'me' insofar as I remember what I said." "It is in memory that the 'I' is constantly present in experience" (Mead, 1934: 174). Through self-observation the individual sees the "me" as a memory of past behavior. "The 'I' is his action ... and it gets into his experience only after he has carried out the act. Then he is aware of it" (Mead, 1934: 175). "The real self that appears in that act awaits the completion of the act itself." "[W]e can catch it in our memory" as a "me" (Mead, 1934: 203). Thus, the "me" is "the reflective self" (Mead, 1913/1964: 145). As we reflect back on our actions, we see the version of our self as object called the "me." "We have to recall the experience to become aware that we have been involved as selves..." (Mead, 1913/1964: 145).

Because self-observation can only reveal the self as an object—always as a "me," and never as the elusive "I"—the existence of the "I" is only inferred from observations on the "me." "Such an 'I' is a presupposition, but never a presentation of conscious experience, for the moment it is presented it has passed into the objective case" and become a "me" (Mead, 1913/1964: 142). Thus, we do not know until after we act what the "I" is, what its actual capacities are. "It is only after we have done the thing that we are going to do that we are aware of what we are doing" (Mead, 1934: 203).

As we can never completely know our own selves or the selves of others, our "explanations" or "accounts" for the behavior of self and others are always to some degree inaccurate. We are always partially unconscious of the nature of our actions. Hence, we need to be cautious about taking people's accounts of behavior at face value.

"The good reasons for which we act and by which we account for our actions are not the real reasons" (Mead, 1938: 480). Our accounts of behavior are constructions based on limited knowledge, and they change as new experiences lead us to reconstruct our conceptions of both past and future events (Mead, 1929b; 1932: 7-9, 24-31).

Creativity and Control. The "I" and the "me" serve different functions, both for the individual and for the society. The "I" is the source of spontaneity and innovative actions. The "me" is the vehicle of self-regulation and social control. The two facets of the self can function smoothly together, though they do not always. Both have their positive values. The "I" is creative. The "me" sets limits and imposes structure based on social values. "The novelty comes in the action of the 'I,' but the structure, the form of the self is one which is conventional," originating from the "me" (Mead, 1934: 209). Because we can never directly observe the "I," we can never be certain exactly what it will do next. "The 'I' is something that is more or less uncertain" (Mead, 1934: 176). The "I" is unpredictable. "That action of the 'I' is something the nature of which we cannot tell in advance" (Mead, 1934: 177). The "I" is a source of the unexpected, the novel, the creative. Thus, "the 'I' gives the sense of freedom, of initiative." "[E]xactly how we will act never gets into experience until after the action takes place" (Mead, 1934: 177-178).

Even if we try to predict the next response of the "I," we are seldom completely successful: Novel and unpredictable responses can appear at any time. "The general conditions under which one is going to act may be present in one's experience, but he is ... ignorant of just how he is going to respond. . ." (Mead, 1934: 197). Even if he "has rehearsed the situation in his own mind," his actual acts may turn out different from those he rehearsed (Mead, 1934: 197). When he first planned what he would say, "he did not know what he was going to say. He then said something that was novel to himself.... Such a novel reply to the social situation ... constitutes the 'I' as over against the 'me.' The 'me' is a conventional, habitual individual" (Mead, 1934: 197); whereas the "I" is the source of novel responses that break away from convention and habitual patterns.

The qualities of the "I" relate closely to Mead's views on emergence. In our world, novel things are always emerging (Mead, 1929a; 1929b; 1932; 1934: 198ff; 1936: 290f, 405f, 414), and the "I" is the source of the emergents in human conduct. Although a person can partially predict the acts of the next moment, "the situation may change, the act may be different from that which the individual himself expected to carry out..." (Mead, 1934: 203). The person "astonishes himself by his conduct as much as he astonishes other people" (Mead, 1934: 204). The novel acts that emerge from the "I" have the potential for surprising us at every turn. There are countless possibilities for novel and creative conduct. "We do not know just what they are. They are in a certain sense the most fascinating contents that we can contemplate..." (Mead, 1934: 204). Whenever we are surprised by our own creative actions, we may realize that we have creative potentials that we cannot perceive (because they belong to the "I" rather than the "me"). It is from "the possibilities of the 'I' . . . that novelty arises and it is there that our most important values are located" (Mead, 1934: 204). In various places, Mead stated that the unique creative contributions of the individual were the most precious qualities of the individual, both for the individual and for the society (Mead, 1929a/1964: 341; 1934: 324; 1936: 405-417). Novel and creative actions add zest and interest to our lives and are the innovations that permit social change and adaptation.

Mead did not describe the "I" as inherently wild or antisocial.[62] The "I" is merely the source of unexpected, emergent acts. Some of these innovations may be valuable, creative contributions that benefit the society; others may be socially useless or deleterious. One of the functions of the "me" is to evaluate the innovations of the "I" from the perspective of society, encouraging socially useful innovations while discouraging undesirable actions. "If we use a Freudian expression, the 'me' is in a certain sense a censor" (Mead, 1934: 210). As a censor, the "me" provides support for the socially useful contributions of the "I" while keeping the problematic facets of the "I" under control.

After the "I" produces either socially desirable or undesirable innovations, these actions enter self-consciousness in terms of the "me." Viewing our acts from the role of others causes us either to approve or to disapprove of those actions, according to social standards. "We are in possession of selves just insofar as we can and do take the attitudes of others toward ourselves and respond to those attitudes. We approve of ourselves and condemn ourselves. We pat ourselves upon the back and in blind fury attack ourselves" (Mead, 1924-25/1964: 288). Our thoughts about the "me" reflect the views of the generalized other—from games and institutions—and give us a form of self-control needed to be good team players and fit into society. The "me" represents "that group of attitudes which stands for others in the community, especially that organized group of responses which we have detailed in discussing the game on the one hand and social institutions on the other" (Mead, 1934: 194).

The self-evaluations of the "me" reflect social values. "The 'me' is essentially a member of a social group, and represents, therefore, the values of the group....Its values are the values that belong to society."

"Without this structure of things, the life of the self would be impossible" (Mead, 1934: 214). In order for society *and the self* (which is derived from society) to function, people must be able to discriminate socially valuable from socially deleterious acts by applying social values to their own actions.

The "me" is the source of social concern. As we reflect on our actions, we ask if we are helping or hurting others. Thus, the "me" provides an internal system of social control. "Social control is the expression of the 'me' over against the expression of the 'I.' It sets the limits..." (Mead, 1934: 210). The type of social control arising from the "me" is "not simply the social control that results from blind habit, but a social control that comes from the individual assuming the same attitude toward himself that the community assumes toward him." "[H]e will recognize what are his duties as well as what are his rights. He takes the attitude of the community toward himself" (Mead, 1936: 377). Thus, social control from the "me" does not operate via unthinking obedience to society. People know their duties and rights and use reflective intelligence to select the best path of action, as they see it from their particular perspective on the social process. At times, reflective intelligence reveals that one's duties to others are more important than one's rights to pursue purely personal interests. At other times, personal rights outweigh duty to others.

Naturally, there is considerable variation among individuals in their motivation and capacity to use the social concern of the "me" to control their own activities according to social values. People's capacity for role taking is one determinant of their use of social values for self-control.

> [I]nsofar as [a person] can assume the organized attitudes of a number [of others] that are cooperating in a common activity, he takes the attitudes of the group toward himself ... [thereby] ... defining the object of the group, that which defines and controls the response. Social control, then, will depend upon the degree to which the individual does assume the attitudes of those in the group who are involved with him in his social activities [Mead, 1924-25/1964: 290].

Thus, there are degrees of self-imposed social control. "Social control depends, then, upon the degree to which the individuals in society are able to assume the attitudes of the others who are involved with them in common endeavor" (Mead, 1924-25/1964: 291). Although many people can control their actions to coordinate with their micro social environment or groups they closely identify with, people often fail to take the role of others and work for the betterment of the larger society and whole international community. The long history of human intergroup hostility and warfare shows that people often prefer to fight others rather than cooperate for the improvement of the larger social system (Mead, 1924-25/1964: 292f).

The type of constraints imposed by the "me" can be influenced by the people around us. Depending on the situation, this can lead to either undesirable or desirable results. The expression of the self can "take place in a form which involves degradation, or in a form which involves the emergence of higher values" (Mead, 1934: 213). When a person is caught up in the activities of an angry mob, the person's "me" may be degraded to a primitive level, allowing the person to express violent impulses that otherwise would have been controlled (Mead, 1934: 213, 218ff). In these cases, the "me" is influenced by others such that it "supports and emphasizes the more violent sort of impulsive expression" (Mead, 1934: 213). Similar things can occur in times of war, when large numbers of people express hostility toward an enemy. Under such strong social influence, an individual's "me" may be reduced to a baser level and hostile impulses can appear without constraint. The unimpeded expression of the "I" is often very exciting: "There is a great deal of exhilaration in situations involved in the hostility of other nations..." (Mead, 1934: 218-219).

In other cases, social influences on an individual's "me" can lead to desirable and gratifying results. For example, we may open up with a friend, blurting out ideas that normally would be guarded and censored by the "me." "There is a satisfaction in letting one's self go in this way. The sort of thing that under other circumstances you would not say and would not even let yourself think is now naturally uttered" (Mead, 1934: 213). In a group of like-minded people, the "me" can also be less guarded, impose fewer constraints, and allow the person to utter things "which may surprise the person himself" (Mead, 1934: 213). This unconstrained expression of the "I" can be beneficial when it allows self-expression with friends and companions.

"I" and "Me" Together. Mead saw society as needing a balance of creative diversity on one hand, and shared meanings and common responses on the other (Mead, 1934: 199, 212, 323-328). The "I" provides the creativity; and the "me" the communalities. A society that encourages people to be creative and different may benefit from those individuals who make creative contributions to art, literature, science, politics, and practical affairs. Nevertheless, for society to function as an integrated whole, all the unique selves must coordinate to some degree. "Society is the interaction of these selves, and an interaction that is only possible if out of their diversity unity arises. We are indefinitely different from each other, but our differences make interaction possible. Society is unity in diversity. However there is always present the danger of its miscarriage" (Mead, 1929c/1964: 359). Too

much diversity can lead to chaos and disorganization. The "me" provides the common interests and social concern that helps people organize their creative diversity in a constructive manner.

People have different mixtures of the strengths of "I" and "me." A person may develop the strengths of the "I" or the "me"—or both, or neither. Some people emphasize one facet of the self—either the "I" or the "me"—more than the other. In order to break away from conventional old patterns and explore creative new alternatives, the artist develops a strong "I" and partially neglects the social conventions of the "me." In the artist or creative person, the "conventional form may be reduced to a minimum." And "the emphasis upon the element of novelty is carried to the limit" (Mead, 1934: 209). In contrast, conservative people develop the "me" more than the "I," guiding their actions to conform to social values and minimize personal deviations from the norm (Mead, 1934: 200).

Mead saw the "I" and "me" functioning smoothly together in the fully developed individual. "Both aspects of the 'I' and 'me' are essential to the self in its full expression" (Mead, 1934: 199). Both "I" and "me" serve important functions and the person benefits from having both well developed. Both the self-expression of "I" and the socially organized work of the "me" are needed for the smooth function of society. "A person who cannot do a certain amount of stereotyped work is not a healthy individual. Both the health of the individual and the stability of society call for a very considerable amount of such work." "Nevertheless ... there must be some way in which the individual can express himself" by original, creative work (Mead, 1934: 212). When a person has the freedom, "he can take over responsibility and carry out things in his own way, with an opportunity to think his own thoughts" (Mead, 1934: 213). Such independence brings "some of the most exciting and gratifying experiences" (Mead, 1934: 213).

Because the "I" can break away from the habitual and the conventional, it is the "I" that allows people to assert their differences from the group. "The demand is freedom from conventions, from given laws" (Mead, 1934: 199). Mead conceived of demands for freedom as a desire to move "from a narrow and restricted community to a larger one, that is, larger in the logical sense of having rights which are not so restricted" (Mead, 1934: 199). In the most desirable form, this involves making constructive contributions that will improve society. However, for an individual to contribute constructively to the group, the individual must coordinate and cooperate with the group if the contribution is to be of use.

What the individual accomplishes must be something that is in itself social. So far as he is a self, he must be an organic part of the life of the

community, and his contribution has to be something that is social. ...
One may be somewhat ahead of his time, but that which he brings forward must belong to the life of the community to which he belongs.
There is, then, a functional difference [between individuals], but it must
be a functional difference which can be entered into in some real sense
by the rest of the community [Mead, 1934: 324].

Mead valued the combination of creativity and social order together.
"The value of an ordered society is essential to our existence, but there
also has to be room for an expression of the individual himself if there
is to be a satisfactorily developed society. A means for such expression
must be provided" (Mead, 1934: 221). Modern Western societies have
been moderately successful in giving people the freedom to express
unique individual qualities. "Primitive human society offers much
less scope for individuality—for original, unique, or creative thinking
and behavior on the part of the individual self..." (Mead, 1934: 221).
Mead argued that primitive societies tended to be more conventional
than modern societies. "The evolution of civilized human society
from primitive human society has largely depended upon or resulted
from a progressive social liberation of the individual self and his conduct" (Mead, 1934: 221). This liberation has resulted, in part, from
the emergence of modern science (Mead, 1936: 405-417). The scientific method places great value on the individual and his or her unique
contributions to solving problems, making scientific discoveries, and
promoting social adaptation. "We are solving problems, and those
problems can appear only in the experience of the individual. It is that
which gives the importance to the individual, gives him a value which
cannot be stated. He has a certain preciousness which cannot be
estimated" (Mead, 1936: 411). To the degree that scientific values influence a society, people are given a range of freedom to develop and
express unique contributions.

* * *

In this and preceding chapters, we have seen the reciprocal interaction of the individual and society. From infancy, society influences
the development of the individual's mind, self, and conduct; as the individual grows up, the individual has an increasing influence on his or her
social and physical environment. The next chapter presents Mead's
views on society and social change.

9

Macro Theory
General

In the preceding chapters we have seen that society played an important role in Mead's theory of the emergence and structure of the mind, self, and human conduct. During the socialization process, individuals acquire symbols, thoughts, and behavior from their society (arrows e and f in Figure 1; see Chapter 1). In turn, the thoughts and actions of these individuals shape the structure and evolution of society (arrows i and j in the figure). One of the great strengths of Mead's theory is its ability to unify societal and individual processes. This and the next chapter focus special attention on Mead's theories of macro society (c in Figure 1), along with its relation to the physical environment (d in the figure).

The macro components of Mead's theoretical system are not as well developed as the micro. This is, in part, due to the fact that Mead began his career focusing mostly on philosophy, social psychology, and micro social topics, only turning detailed attention to macro issues in his later decades.[63] Also, because he was a philosopher, he was not as close to and familiar with the methods, data, and theory on macro as were social scientists who had specialized on macro topics. Nevertheless, macro societal structures and processes are essential components of his theory. In order to construct a unified theoretical system that reveals the interactions of all components of the social process, empirical data and theories on macro phenomena must be integrated with data and theories on biology, social psychology, and environmental variables. One cannot fully understand the workings of any subset of the system until data and theories on all components of the system have been merged into a unified theoretical system. Macro societal data and theory are just as important as information on other parts of the whole model.

This chapter presents Mead's general views on social evolution and change; and the next presents his theories about specific macro phenomena. Both chapters demonstrate how Mead dealt with macro phenomena in ways that facilitate the construction of unified theories. Unlike some social theorists, Mead developed macro theories that did not place barriers between macro and micro levels of social analysis; and his work can be a model for contemporary social scientists who are interested in building unified theories.

SOCIAL EVOLUTION

Mead drew heavily on theories of biological evolution in his analysis of society and social change (Mead, 1899; 1908; 1910a; 1923; 1924-25; 1927b; 1929-30; 1934: 214f, 250ff; 1936: 127ff, 145-168, 270ff, 288ff, 301ff, 364-384, 411; 1938: 496f, 503f, 508f, 512, 515f). However, he did not accept the idealized model of evolution that some social theorists have adopted. The idealized view of biological evolution interprets the fossil record as showing the emergence of organisms of ever-increasing complexity and sophistication, suggesting that progress is a natural consequence of evolution. In addition, the highly functional nature of the heart, lungs, eyes, brain, and other structures is often used to support the idealistic theory that all structures have evolved to function adaptively within the whole organism.

Mead rejected these idealized conceptions of evolution. He did not assume that progress was inevitable or that structures were necessarily functional.

Progress. History provides data on the evolution of human societies, and some theorists have used historical data as evidence that societies are naturally evolving toward improved conditions. However, as Mead explained, people did not always have this belief in progress (Mead, 1938: 494-519). The ancient Greeks and Romans did not interpret history in terms of progress. "The notion of progress was meaningless for Greek society..." (Mead, 1934: 294). In Greek and Roman society, "values existed fully realized, if not in the sensible world, in the supersensible world of ideas and forms" (Mead, 1938: 504-505). However, "a philosophy of history arose as soon as men conceived that society was moving toward the realization of triumphant ends in some great far-off event" (Mead, 1938: 504). In Western history, the first version of the great event was the salvation of all

humankind and the realization of God's perfect world. Once an idealistic future condition was conceptualized it was easy to interpret
history as moving toward that end. "It's earliest form was in Paul's
belief in the coming of the Lord within the lifetime of his own generation. By the time of Augustine these hopes had sunk into a dateless
night" (Mead, 1938: 504). Nevertheless, the early Christian theologians continued to think that the perfect ideal would eventually arise,
and generally their "philosophy of history was some variant upon the
plan of salvation" (Mead, 1938: 505).

By the Renaissance, scientific advances were being coupled with the
Christian world view (Mead, 1938: 513), leading to the notion of
human progress on earth as people gained increasing control over
nature: "An earthly goal was pictured in Sir Thomas More's *Utopia*
and in Bacon's *New Atlantis*" (Mead, 1938: 505). A few centuries
later, Hegel developed an idealistic philosophy that described a dialec-
tical process that was supposed to produce inevitable progress toward
the ideal Christian state.[64] "Hegel presents human progress as a finite
temporal process that ceaselessly advances toward a goal at infinity,
the divine timeless absolute..." (Mead, 1938: 505).

In contrast, Mead postulated no ideal state toward which evolution
is moving.

> Scientific method has no vision, given in the mount, of a perfected order
> of society, but it does carry with it the assumption that the intelligence
> which exhibits itself in the solution of problems in natural science is of
> the same character as that which we apply or should apply in dealing
> with our social and moral problems. . . [Mead, 1923/1964: 264].

"We do not know what sort of society or what sort of men are
ultimately desirable. We can only feel our way in finding out what is
desirable. Now, that may be done in a haphazard fashion or it may be
done in a systematic procedure" (Mead, 1938: 509). Although Mead
clearly advocated the use of systematic scientific methods (rather than
haphazard methods) for selecting future social practices (Mead, 1899/
1936: 360-385), he did not claim that the scientific approach would
carry us toward some ideal and predictable outcomes. "It is impossible to so forecast any future condition that depends upon the evolution of society as to be able to govern our conduct by such a forecast"
(Mead, 1899/1964: 3). Because novel and unpredictable events are
always emerging, the future is inherently unknowable. "It is always
the unexpected that happens. . . ." "In the social world we must recognize the working hypothesis as the form into which all theories must be
cast as completely as in the natural sciences" (Mead, 1899/1964: 3).
Thus, scientific theories of society are "only provisionally true" (Mead,
1899/1964: 3).

We know that society is in a process of evolution, though we do not know what forms of institutions, of monuments and products ... will supervene. We know that we are on the way, though we do not know where we are going. In other words, we have a different philosophy of history from that of the medievalist or the Elizabethan [Mead, 1938: 503].

Although Mead wrote about progress, he did not define progress as movement toward an ideal state or condition. "It has often been pointed out, of course, that evolution does not reach any goal" (Mead, 1936: 372). Mead defined progress merely as effective problem solving. "Progress, as I have pointed out, even from the point of view of evolution, is the constant meeting of problems and solving them" (Mead, 1936: 411). Compared with the societies of earlier nonscientific periods of history, modern Western societies have a relatively strong commitment to scientific and democratic problem solving. As a consequence, the idea of "progress is dominantly characteristic of modern society or civilization, by virtue of the distinctive organization of the modern state which is sufficiently flexible to be able to cope, to some extent at least, with the social conflicts among individuals that arise within it..." (Mead, 1934: 294).

Mead's appraisal that reflective intelligence and science are the best methods we have for problem solving did not lead him to assume that reflective and empirical methods could resolve all problems. Although he stated in places that science has given us a great deal of power to solve problems and control the environment (Mead, 1936: 261f, 372f), he also pointed out how hard it is to solve societal problems, such as avoiding war, making democracy work, improving the criminal justice system, and so forth (Mead, 1913; 1917-18; 1923). Thus, progress— defined as effective problem solving—is not inevitable. Nor did Mead anticipate a speedy solution to social problems even if we were to seriously apply our intelligence to the task. "I am not so silly as to suppose that, if we were simply willing to be intelligent, we could in the immediate future solve any of these fundamental social problems" (Mead, 1938: 490).

Functional Analysis. Idealized models of evolution often create the impression that evolution naturally produces highly adaptive and functional structures. For example, during biological evolution, the heart, kidneys, brain, eyes, and other organs have been molded into highly adaptive and functional structures, each organ contributing importantly to the survival of the whole organism.[65] By analogy, idealistic social theorists often treat human societies as if each social structure within the whole society has evolved to an adaptive level, carrying out its specific functions within the social whole. This tends to be a conservative view. The assumption that social structures are adaptive and functional makes it easy to overlook social problems and the need for social change.

Mead's version of functional analysis reflects his rejection of idealistic philosophy and his adoption of a purely empirical, pragmatic view. For Mead, social structures are best analyzed in terms of their *functional value* in the society: How well does the social structure function in the society? The functional value of any social structure was an empirical question: Does the criminal justice system function in a problem-free manner? In what ways does it function well? What are its faults? These questions can be asked of any social structure. This method helps locate problems rather than obscuring them with idealistic assumptions. Once aware of social problems, we can use reflective intelligence and science to attempt to resolve the problems and improve the functioning of the social system.

Rather than assuming that organisms and social structures have evolved to an adaptive, functional state, Mead emphasized that evolution occurs in response to continuously arising problems (Mead, 1923; 1932; 1936).[66] Problems rather than perfect adaptation are the center of focus. In addition, problems reveal the degree to which various social structures and practices have functional value. "There are no absolute values." "There is only one field within which the estimation [of values] can be made, and that is within the actual problem" (Mead, 1923/1964: 262). When people and institutions with different values come into conflict, how can we gain a clear understanding of the relevant values? "They ought to be defined by the conflict out of which the problem has arisen." "[V]alues define themselves definitely enough when they are brought into conflict with each other. So facts define themselves in scientific problems" (Mead, 1923/1964: 260). From the scientific and pragmatic point of view, the best values are those that are consistent with the selection of the most functional social practices and institutions.[67] "It is to this task that a scientifically trained intelligence must insistently devote itself, that of stating, just as far as possible, our institutions, our social habits and customs, in terms of what they are to do, in terms of their functions" (Mead, 1923/1964: 262).

Not only did Mead reject the idealistic view that social institutions are naturally functional, he explained how institutions that are *not* functional can persist in society (in spite of their lack of function).

An institution should arise and be kept alive by its own function, but insofar as it does not function, the ideal of it can be kept alive only by

some cult, whose aim is not the functioning of the institution, but the
continued presence of the idea of it in the minds of those that cherish it
[Mead, 1923/1964: 259].

For example, members of a religious cult may value their cult in spite
of the general societal opinion that the cult is dangerous. In fact,
various institutions[68] are maintained by idealistic groups, even though
the institutions fail to have functional value.

Mead described the values of those cults that maintain nonfunc-
tional institutions as "cult values" and contrasted them with the functional values of institutions, which are effective in resolving problems
and improving social conditions (Mead, 1923; 1934: 296). Cult values
tend to be conservative. "The religion gathered about the cult ... is
more conservative than almost any other institution in the community"
(Mead, 1934: 296). In contrast, functional values are oriented to solving problems, making things work, advancing to meet new problems,
and adjusting to deal with ever-changing conditions. Mead advocated
replacing cult values (which are either useless or deleterious) with
functional values. The scientific approach accepts "human society as
a part of the natural order ... and with it comes the demand, that just
as far as possible we substitute functional values for cult values in
formulating and undertaking to solve our social problems" (Mead,
1923/1964: 264-265). Although cult values may seem reasonable to
those within the cult, their limitations are seen when the cult's functioning is evaluated within the larger system of interdependent social
structures. "The task of intelligence is to use this growing consciousness of [social] interdependence to formulate the problems of
all, in terms of the problem of everyone. Insofar as this can be accomplished cult values will pass over into functional values" (Mead,
1923/1964: 264).

All institutions are interdependent, and the goal of a pragmatic
social science is to improve the function of each institution within the
whole. "The mere recitation of [the] essential social institutions ex-
hibits their vital relationship with one another." "No one institution
could stand by itself, and the development of each one of them has
been the outcome of the processes of all of them" (Mead, 1938: 496).

Viewing institutions as interdependent does not imply that institutions naturally interact in a harmonious manner. Medieval Christian
theologians created an idealistic view of society in which all institutions were pictured as fitting into one harmonious, unified system.
"All the values which these institutions have enshrined could be con-
templated as but the phases of a single *summum bonum,* the glory of
God. Everything, including our values, was placed with such ideal

neatness in the *Summa* of a Thomas Aquinas" (Mead, 1938: 497). Although moderns may sometimes "look back with a certain nostalgia to the thirteenth century" (Mead, 1938: 497) and wish for such a harmonious social system (if it ever existed), Mead readily admitted that modern society is not a smoothly functioning system: It is "not an organic whole" (Mead, 1938: 497). Instead, we live in a pluralistic society, with conflicts between different institutions and groups. "Each social institution with the good that it subtends asserts and maintains itself but finds itself in that assertion in conflict with other institutions and their goods" (Mead, 1938: 498). Although modern society is rife with conflicts, Mead stated that "unless men simply run amuck" we must recognize the basic functions that are essential, "and these functions must persist even if the values which the institutions mediate find themselves in conflict" (Mead, 1938: 498).

The preceding points make it clear that Mead's form of functional analysis is quite different from the types of "functionalism" based on idealistic philosophies. Although Mead made passing references to people and institutions as being "organs" that carry out functions within the larger "social organism" (Mead, 1927a: 152, 169; 1934: 292), he recognized that those functions were often not carried out well and that there existed serious problems preventing adaptive social function. Mead rejected idealistic assumptions and methods, opting instead for a purely scientific approach. "The problems of social theory must be research problems" (Mead, 1923/1964: 262-263). He advocated using the methods "of experimental science, by means of which men change the environment within which society exists, and the forms and institutions of society itself" (Mead, 1938: 508).

Mead was aware that many people were reluctant to apply scientific methods to controlling social conditions. "We still hesitate to state our problems in terms of these conditions [of scientific control] because of the fear of weakening or invalidating old values which are consecrated by the past, and because of the responsibility which the new statement of the problem carries with it" (Mead, 1938: 493). The responsibility of a truly pragmatic, scientific approach to society and social change is enormous, because it requires a careful evaluation of all facets of the whole social system (Mead, 1908; 1917; 1923; 1938: 460-465).

Cooperation and Criticism. Mead's approach to social change and function demonstrates the value of both supporting functional practices and institutions *and* criticizing defective ones. Both types of conduct are needed to maintain and advance functional values. When acting within a functional institution, we should listen to the voice of the group and cooperate for social goals. However, when there are problems, criticism is in order. "Both must be there: the voice of the community and our own; the ordered community that endows us with its rights and its obligations, and ourselves that approve or dissent" (Mead, 1930/1964: 395).

First, the socially responsible person should value and support functional practices. For example, Mead considered that people have a right to keep private possessions and property. Therefore, it was functional for institutions to maintain people's rights of possession. It follows that, when dealing with other people's possessions, the individual "must be honorable and respect property, because this is the voice of the entire community and he must obey in order to live in it" (Mead, 1927a: 150). The person who cannot cooperate with others, conform to generally beneficial social conventions, and function as a responsible member of society may be deprived of his or her rights and freedoms. Social living "brings responsibility with it" (Mead, 1927a: 150). "Rights and obligations go together. . . . This is the imperative character of conduct, which springs ultimately from the social situation" (Mead, 1927a: 151).

However, we are not obligated to conform to social practices that are problematic. Problems are the natural impetus for critical thinking, reflective intelligence, and problem solving. Although Eastern religions suppress the self and social criticism, "we, on the contrary, attack society and try to produce a better society instead of suppressing the self..." (Mead, 1927a: 151). When societal conditions are problematic, people can reflect "critically ... upon the organized social structure of the society ... and ... reorganize or reconstruct or modify that social structure..." (Mead, 1934: 308). "We can reform the order of things; we can insist on making the community standards better standards. We are not simply bound by the community." "That is the way, of course, in which society gets ahead. . . . We are continually changing our social system in some respects, and we are able to do that intelligently because we can think" (Mead, 1934: 168). "We are exerting ourselves, bringing forward our own opinion, criticizing the attitudes of others, and approving or disapproving" (Mead, 1934: 180). "An individual is constantly reacting to such an organized community in the way of expressing himself, not necessarily asserting himself in the offensive sense but expressing himself, being himself in such a co-operative process as belongs to any community" (Mead, 1934: 197-198). In essence, criticism of social problems is a form of social cooperation if it is oriented toward improving the functioning of society.

For Mead, the decision either to comply with or to criticize any social practice should be based on reflective intelligence. Because it is a social decision that can influence the lives of others, it is a moral decision and must be made responsibly. For Mead the "moral dictum" controlling all social decisions is that people use reflective intelligence to understand and evaluate *all* the concerns surrounding each choice, then to select the one with the greatest functional value (Mead, 1908/1964: 87f). "What is of importance is that all the interests which are involved should come to expression" (Mead, 1915/1964: 166). It is crucial that we allow "all the interests that are involved in the issue at stake to come to the surface and be adequately estimated" (Mead, 1915/1964: 166). Not only should all the options be considered at an abstract level, we should attempt to gain a concrete understanding of how our decisions will influence others (Mead, 1914: 93-105). "We should not forget that the ultimate guarantee [of wise choices] must be found in the reaction of men and women to a human situation so fully presented that their whole natures respond" (Mead, 1915/1964: 170).

Evolution or Revolution? Mead believed that it was functional for societies to be able to change to cope with any problems or novel conditions that emerge over time (Mead, 1899; 1936: 364, 405-417). However, change that does not conserve valuable past contributions is not functional. Thus, there needs to be a balance between conserving the good from the past and changing the bad. The problem of society is the following: "How can you present order and structure in society and yet bring about the changes that need to take place, are taking place?" (Mead, 1936: 361).

Mead's historical analysis of Western society (Mead, 1936) revealed that "the control over community life in the past has been ... almost inevitably conservative" (Mead, 1936: 361). Conservative social order and control are not without value; however, society also needs methods for making adaptive changes.

> The first step consciously taken in advance of this position is that which grew out of the French Revolution, that which in a certain sense incorporated the principle of revolution into institutions. That is, when you set up a constitution and one of the articles in it is that the constitution may be changed, then you have, in a certain sense, incorporated the very process of revolution into the order of society [Mead, 1936: 361].

If this type of system works as designed, you do not have to overthrow the entire constitution and government in order to modify specific parts of the system.

Planned social change can be based on idealism or science. Hegel, Marx,[69] and other idealistic thinkers believed that an ideal future design of society could be known, and that this knowledge could provide reliable guidelines for planned social change. Mead argued that *no* theory could predict the long-term future condition of society or provide reliable information about an ideal future design of society (Mead, 1899; 1936: 215-242). Given the fact that novel, unexpected events are always emerging, it is impossible to make accurate predictions far into the future (Mead, 1899; 1932; 1936: 236-242, 281-291). Hence, idealistic theories are quite misleading. "Every attempt to direct conduct by a fixed idea of the world of the future must be, not only a failure, but also pernicious" (Mead, 1899/1964: 5). The continuous emergence of unexpected events and problems requires frequent readjustment of social institutions and practices, along with our theories about them.[70] Thus, we need more flexible methods for understanding and guiding social change than are provided by idealistic models.

Mead argued that the scientific method was superior to idealistic approaches for studying society and its problems. Science provides a method for analyzing social problems, designing and testing new practices, thereby suggesting empirically defensible forms of social change (Mead, 1899; 1936). Scientific means of changing society are well suited to dealing with unexpected new problems as they arise, while making no claims about distant future ideals. "What we have is a method ... not an ideal to work toward" (Mead, 1899/1964: 3). The scientific method is well suited for advancing social evolution by the use of careful, systematic selection rather than haphazard, or "natural" selection.[71] "[T]he scientific method, as such, is, after all, only the evolutionary process grown self-conscious" (Mead, 1936: 364, 371). "Societies develop, just as animal forms develop by adjusting themselves to the problems that they find before them." "Science comes in to aid society in getting a method of progress." "This sort of method enables us to keep the order of society and yet to change that order within the process itself" (Mead, 1936: 365-366). Retaining the good while changing the bad is basically an evolutionary strategy based on gradual, piecemeal change rather than revolution. Although social change via scientific methods is slower than revolution, it is faster than haphazard evolutionary change and more efficient than either revolution or haphazard evolution.

ECOLOGY

Approaching the study of society with a strong grounding in biological and evolutionary theories, Mead was aware that ecological variables (involving the entire organic and inorganic environment) are crucial in explaining the evolution of species and societies (Mead, 1934: 245). Species change and evolve as their environment changes: For example, after the onset of the ice age, "the woolly elephant [and] the hairy hippopotamus ... were adjustments to a new environment" (Mead, 1936: 128). Societies also change as ecological situations change, problems arise, and people grapple with them (Mead, 1934: 215f).

Some evolutionary models describe living organisms as having a passive role in the evolutionary process, being molded in ways that are completely determined by environmental conditions. "On this view the individual is really passive as over against the influences which are affecting it all the time. But what needs now to be recognized is that the character of the organism is a determinant of its environment" (Mead, 1934: 215). Mead rejected the view that the organism is passive and emphasized that the "determining relationship is bilateral" (Mead, 1938: 412). "That reaction is not simply a determination of the organism by the environment, since the organism determines the environment as fully as the environment determines the organs" (Mead, 1934: 129). The organism actively modifies its own environment. "The situation is one in which there is action and reaction, and adaptation that changes the form [of life] must also change the environment" (Mead, 1934: 215; see also Mead, 1922/1964: 241). "Since organism and environment determine each other and are mutually dependent for their existence, it follows that the life-process, to be adequately understood, must be considered in terms of their interrelations" (Mead, 1934: 130).

On one side of the bilateral determining relationship, people partially determine their own environment (Mead, 1934: 214ff, 245-248). First, through selective attention, we focus on only selected portions of the environment; thus we determine which part of the environment will occupy our attention, thoughts, and plans for action. Also, the ways in which we describe and explain the environment allow us to create countless symbolic representations of the environment. "Our environment exists in a certain sense as hypotheses" (Mead, 1934: 247). And of course, the way we describe the environment greatly influences the way we respond to it. Finally, much as other animals, we act on the environment, construct things in it, and thereby change it (Mead, 1934: 247f). "The striking thing about the human organism is the elaborate extension of control of [this] type" (Mead, 1934: 248). We build vast cities, transport water across great distances, grow the plants that provide the best harvests, and so forth (Mead, 1927a: 116; 1934: 249ff; 1936: 250f, 260ff, 372; 1938: 508). "The development of human society on a larger scale has led to a very complete control of its environment" (Mead, 1934: 249).

On the other side of the bilateral determining relationship, we must recognize that the environment is a partial determinant of the types of problems we face and the way we solve them. For example, the appearance of a new disease creates problems for us to solve. As we develop hypotheses about the disease, we submit these hypotheses to be tested by their effectiveness in dealing with the environment, which then determines which hypotheses are supported and which are not. "Science is tested by the success of its postulates" (Mead, 1936: 258). We can create countless numbers of hypotheses[72] about a new disease and ways to control it, but only those hypotheses that work—that is, have pragmatic, functional value—are worth keeping. Thus, the environment determines which theories and practices are discarded and which are retained for further development.

Mead was aware that the bilateral relationship between people and their environment must also affect society.[73]

> As a man adjusts himself to a certain environment he becomes a different individual; but in becoming a different individual he has affected the community in which he lives. It may be a slight effect, but in so far as he has adjusted himself, the adjustments have changed the type of the environment to which he can respond and the world is accordingly a different world. There is always a mutual relationship of the individual and the community in which the individual lives [Mead, 1934: 215].

When a person adjusts to the environment, the impact of this action on society may be large or small;[74] it "may be desirable or it may be undesirable, but it inevitably takes place" (Mead, 1934: 216).

Thus, human behavior and society are not simply passive products of evolutionary processes, determined by ecological variables. We have always exercised control over our environment, and we have the potential to exercise this control much more wisely in the future (Mead, 1936: 250f, 260ff). As already discussed, Mead saw science as the highest form of reflective intelligence and the best method for continually adjusting to new conditions (Mead, 1936: 290). Not only does science allow humans to adjust to their changing environment, it "is an instrument by means of which mankind, the community, gets control over its environment" (Mead, 1936: 360). As we gain increasing control over the environment and the key determinants of natural selection, we will gain increasing control over our own evolution. "It is this control of its own evolution which is the goal of the development of human society" (Mead, 1934: 251). Although Mead was optimistic that humanity could use science to control its own environment and evolution, he did not expect that a stable, functional relationship between the environment and human behavior and society would be attained soon. "We are so far away from any actual final adjustment of this sort that we correctly say that the evolution of the social organism has a long road ahead of it" (Mead, 1934: 252).

Although Mead did not develop the ecological facets of his theory as well as he developed other parts, he did provide the basic theoretical structure that shows how people, society, and the environment inter-act—each influencing the other. In the past two or three decades, it has become abundantly clear that human activities and technologies are having increasing impact on ecological and social systems, making us aware of the interdependence of all parts of the system. Mead's theoretical system that integrates physiology, behavior, society, and ecology in one unified model offers a useful tool for interweaving ecological variables into sociological theories.[75]

* * *

Mead's approach to macro society is based in large part on evolu-tionary models, but it is significantly different from the evolutionary views used by more idealistic social scientists. Mead did not assume that social evolution inevitably led to progress or produced completely adaptive and functional structures. Nor did he assume that human behavior and society were passive elements in the evolutionary equation, being molded in ways that are completely determined by environ-mental factors. The process of social evolution involves a bilat-eral relationship between people and their environment; and increas-ing use of reflective intelligence and science should allow humans to gain ever greater control of the whole process. By criticizing society's faults and cooperating with others to develop more functional alter-natives, we can hasten the evolution of better social conditions and more functional relations with the ecological systems.

10

Macro Theory
Specifics

Mead analyzed several major social institutions, including science, economics, religion, criminal justice, democracy, and other forms of government (Mead, 1914: 78-102; 1917; 1917-18; 1923; 1929-30; 1932; 1934: 281-328; 1936; 1938: 494-519).[76] An overview of these analyses reveals both his methods of approach to and theories about several specific macro phenomena.

Mead's method of macro analysis involved drawing on all empirical disciplines—such as history, [77] anthropology,[78] sociology, economics, social psychology, and biology—relevant to a given topic. As Mead sought to develop a unified empirical system that synthesized data on all facets of the social process, it is not surprising that his explanations of societal phenomena incorporated data from all relevant empirical disciplines. He also recognized the value of realistic art forms and the media for obtaining a concrete understanding of social structures and of people in different sectors of society and different parts of the world (Mead, 1914: 97-102; 1924-25/1964: 292; 1925-26/1964: 301ff; 1934: 257; 1936: 405-417).

Not only did Mead integrate many sources of empirical information in his macro analyses, he was critical of attempts to explain societal processes in terms of variables that reflected only a limited portion of the social whole. For example, Mead criticized the narrowness of economic and hedonistic theories, because each one attempted to explain complex social phenomena in terms of a limited number of variables that did not reflect the entire social process (Mead, 1914: 96-102). "The economic man does not exist separately, his interests cannot be stated in terms of psychology and economics but in terms of the social process as a whole to which this economic process is essential. But the economic process is subsidiary, just as the pleasure and pain are subsidiary'' (Mead, 1914: 96). Any analysis that neglects the ''social process as a whole'' is likely to be inadequate and misleading. It creates an abstraction that fails to deal with the workings of the whole social system. ''The method of overcoming abstractions [such as economic theory] is the integration that takes the economic process over into the whole social process. It is when you get the function of the economic process that it ceases to be a barrier between different sorts of social goods, and it becomes a legitimate technique'' (Mead, 1914: 97). Seeing how economic processes (or any other limited subsystems) are integrated within the whole social process allows us to escape the narrowness of overly specialized theories and integrate their contributions into a larger, unified explanatory system.

The following sections summarize Mead's theories about punitive justice and social organization. The first analysis is brief and provides a clear example of many of Mead's core interests. The second deals with the evolution of social organization from primitive small scale societies to modern society, and involves many more variables than does the first analysis.

PUNITIVE JUSTICE

Mead's analysis of punitive justice systems reveals much of his strategy of approach to institutions and societal practices (Mead, 1917-1918; see also Mead, 1923/1964: 261; 1936: 368-372; 1938: 488). First, he prefaced his most detailed essay on justice systems by tracing the evolution of behavior back to either hostile or friendly instincts (Mead, 1917-18/1964: 213). His analysis indicated that the justice system arose from and is based on hostile instincts. Although the most primitive response to crime was pure hostility, the emergence of courts and legal systems has produced institutions that use reflective processes to control the basic instincts, lifting them above the purely instinctual level. Nevertheless, punitive justice still reveals the operation of hostile impulses and attitudes. Mead attempted to demonstrate that a justice system based on hostile feelings creates serious social problems, and he suggested more functional ways of dealing with crime.

Mead speculated on the history of the punitive response to crime. ''On the evolutionary side, you go back to a situation, we will say, of blood vengeance. A man from one clan kills a man from another. Immediately there arises within the injured clan a man who is determined to revenge the death by killing someone from the other clan, and the next of kin sets out to kill the slayer'' (Mead, 1936: 368). This ''sets up a vicious circle in which the punishment of one murder leads to another.... Out of this arose a method of rude justice, the court, with the taking-over of the administration of justice, of its own assessment of the crime and a penalty that should attach to it" (Mead, 1936: 146). In the early criminal codes, "hostility shows itself in the use of the death penalty for comparatively slight offenses. It is taking the hostile attitude toward the criminal that accounts for the notion that someone must suffer for a crime" (Mead, 1914: 91).

In the later evolution of systems of criminal justice, an attempt was made to "fit the penalty more definitely to what is felt to be the character of the crime" (Mead, 1936: 368). In the Middle Ages, "when courts of justice were the antechambers to chambers of torture, the emphasis lay upon the nice proportioning of the suffering to the offense" (Mead, 1917-18/1964: 217).

> In the older, medieval state the community was called together to witness the suffering of the individual who was being punished.... In our criminal law we have this motive of exacting suffering, and we have a partially worked out theory which states that where a person has committed a crime he should pay by a certain amount of suffering for the wrong he has done.... We fit the punishment to the crime [Mead, 1936: 369].

This type of retributive justice provides a controlled means of expressing the hostility that the community feels toward the criminal. As the justice system evolved in the West, there was an increasing emphasis on crime prevention; but retribution continued to play an important role in the justice system (Mead, 1917-18/1964: 217f). If the justice system functioned well and did not create problems, we might have little reason to be critical of it. "But we know that that process does not work at all" (Mead, 1936: 369). "It is supposed to prevent crime, but it does not prevent it" (Mead, 1923/1964: 261).

Next, Mead evaluated the functional values and problems of the justice system (Mead, 1917-18/1964: 219ff). One function of the justice system is to defend society from offenders. Another is to express "the attitude of hostility to the lawbreaker as an enemy to the society...." This is a way of "satisfying the hostile impulse" (Mead, 1917-18/1964: 221). The court's attack against the criminal offender is conducted much as if the state were doing battle against an enemy. One of the key functions of expressing hostility toward an enemy is the creation of group solidarity (Mead, 1917-18/1964: 222). Hostility toward an enemy strengthens social bonds within a group, giving people a "sense of group solidarity because in the common attack upon the common enemy the individual differences are obliterated" (Mead, 1917-18/1964: 215-216). Although Mead often acknowledged the ability of hostility toward an enemy to produce group solidarity, "the price paid for this solidarity of feeling is great and at times disastrous"(Mead, 1917-18/1964: 229). The use of hostility can lead to a variety of social problems such as mob consciousness, upheavals of patriotism, warfare, and other destructive practices (Mead, 1917-18/1964: 237). "Successful competition in its sharpest form eliminates its competitor" (Mead, 1917-18/1964: 237). Destroying others is not the way to create functional social relations, in which people cooperate for the betterment of society. Mead advocated more cooperative forms of social interaction for building cohesive and functional societies (Mead, 1917-18/1964: 216, 230ff, 238f).

Even though the emphasis on making the criminal suffer may generate some social solidarity, it has distracted us from the more functional value of reinstating "the criminal as a law-abiding citizen" (Mead, 1917-18/1964: 224). The justice system is "based upon defense and not upon function" (Mead, 1917-18/1964: 224).[79]

> Hostility toward the lawbreaker inevitably brings with it the attitudes of retribution, repression, and exclusion. These provide no principles for the eradication of crime, for returning the delinquent to normal social relations, nor for stating the transgressed rights and institutions in terms of their positive social functions [Mead, 1917-18/1964: 226-227].

In addition, repressive institutions (such as the criminal justice system) have a repressive effect on society as a whole, causing many people to abstain from useful creative endeavors for fear of becoming entangled in legal problems. "Just in proportion as we organize by hostility do we suppress individuality" (Mead, 1917-18/1964: 228).

Are there more positive and functional ways in which people can organize society without reliance on hostility? In various contexts, Mead explained how economic relations, trade, science, art, literature, charity, and related institutions provide constructive alternatives to institutions based on hostility (Mead, 1914: 97-102; 1917-18/1964: 229f, 238; 1924-25/1964: 292; 1925-26/1964: 301ff; 1934: 282-305; 1930; 1936). For example, economic and trade relations bring people into cooperative exchange relations that foster communication, role taking with others, and mutual understanding (Mead, 1934: 282-305). The scientific community provides a model of cooperative relations, in which rivalries and hostilities are held within limits by the necessities of cooperative interaction (Mead, 1917-18/1964: 229f).

Turning specifically to the question of crime, Mead suggested some possible alternatives to a punitive system based on hostile attitudes. For example, he noted that the juvenile court had already begun to deal with crime without "the paraphernalia of hostile procedure" (Mead, 1917-18/1964: 231). If the habitual response of showing hostility to the criminal were not controlled, this "social habit ... would condemn the child to the penitentiary and thus make a confirmed

criminal out of him. But it is possible to modify those habits by what
we call the 'scientific method'" (Mead, 1936: 364). Under the influence of modern scientific thinking, we have brought the psychologist, medical officer, and social worker in to help the juvenile offender, family, and neighborhood work together toward reinstating
the juvenile into a more functional relationship with society (Mead,
1917-18/1964: 231). Although the juvenile justice system is far from
perfect, by "centering interest upon reinstatement [it strengthens]
... the sense of forward-looking moral responsibility" (Mead,
1917-18/1964: 231). It emphasizes positive, functional social values,
such as the value "of family relations, of schools, of training of all sorts,
of opportunities to work, and of all the other factors that go to make
up that which is worthwhile in the life of a child or an adult" (Mead,
1917-18/1964: 231). "They are the ends that should determine conduct" (Mead, 1917-18/1964: 232). Although Mead did not promise
any easy solutions to the problems of adult crime, he advocated scientific research oriented toward integrating the criminal into functional
social roles.[80]

SOCIAL ORGANIZATION

Mead traced the evolution of social organization from small-scale,
primitive societies to modern times. Again a central theme is that
society has the potential for functional organization—a potential that
can be realized if we minimize hostility and cooperate to solve social
problems.

Primitive Society. Mead assumed that the most primitive form of
human social organization is the family (Mead, 1914: 80; 1934: 229).
Early small-scale societies were organized around family relations.
Tribal societies are extensions of the family. In addition, "all such
larger units or forms of human social organization as the clan or the
state are ultimately based upon, and (whether directly or indirectly)
are developments from or extensions of, the family" (Mead,
1934: 229).

The family, which is the basic unit of reproduction in the society,
arises from several "fundamental socio-physiological impulses or
needs"[81] that are inherently more friendly than hostile (Mead, 1934:
228). Most important of these are the "sex or reproductive impulse"
the "parental impulse" and the "impulse or attitude of neighborliness, which is a kind of generalization of the parental impulse or attitude and upon which all cooperative social behavior is more or less
dependent" (Mead, 1934: 228-229). These friendly impulses predis-

pose the members of a primitive tribe or clan to cooperate in carrying out functional roles needed for survival and reproduction.

Mead presented several reasons why small-scale, primitive societies based on family relations, though not problem free, tend to have rather functional organization and limited hostility within the group. In primitive societies, "we find the social relationship such that the social ... instincts, both positive and negative [friendly and hostile], are so organized that they lead to balanced and controlled social conduct" (Mead, 1914: 82). This balance arises from the individual's ability to take the role of all the other members in the small-scale society. "When one places himself in the role of another, the conflicting tendencies or instincts are so brought into relationship with each other that we get social control" (Mead, 1914: 82). If one member of the family is angry at a second, the first person can take the role of the second, understand the second's actions, feel sympathy, and thereby bring the hostility impulse under control. Because the group is small, each individual can have concrete, face-to-face relations with all others. Thus, "in the primitive group the person can enter into sympathetic relationship with every member of the group" (Mead, 1914: 82). Also, because the family is based on parental and helping impulses, these kindly impulses help inhibit and control hostile impulses. "Within the group the hostility has been organized so that these instincts lead to competition and rivalry" rather than serious harm (Mead, 1914: 105). Thus, Mead described the small-scale, primitive society as basically a functional and cooperative unit.

Larger Societies. Although role taking, sympathy, and friendly impulses usually kept hostility under control within the small-scale society, these constraints did not operate strongly enough to inhibit hostility toward strangers or between groups that were not linked by family bonds and close face-to-face relations. In addition, there was a predisposition to show hostility to the outsider, as this functioned to strengthen group solidarity. "Over against the individual outside the group is the attitude of hostility, the instinct of injuring" (Mead, 1914: 105). Hostility sometimes merely kept groups at a distance, but it also could lead to blood vengeance and warfare between groups. When hostility led to war, people sought to annihilate their enemies, or make them slaves, and take their lands and possessions. Through this process, some groups grew in size, while gaining increasing land, slaves, and power, until they emerged as empires. These societies—such as the "empires of the valleys of the Nile, the Tigris, and the Euphrates"—were based on war and dominance, rather than on the friendly relations of the family (Mead, 1934: 284).

Warfare and the taking of slaves led to the origins of social stratification based on castes. "The earliest caste is a slave caste. The slave is an outsider, yet he is looked upon as the possession of an individual. He is robbed of the social status of the other members of the group because he is looked upon as an enemy" (Mead, 1914: 83).[82] The relations between castes based on hostility are thus quite different from those within the family, which are based on friendliness and function. "In a community that is comparatively small, difference of function does not carry with it a caste distinction but a more vivid sympathy..." (Mead, 1914: 84-85). With the emergence of castes, people felt hostility—rather than sympathy—for people in other castes (even though they felt sympathy and friendly feelings for family and close relations within their own social stratum).

Increase in social size and the social distance between slaves and citizens decreased the direct, face-to-face contact needed for concrete understanding of others, which further impeded role taking and reduced sympathy. With increasing social size, "we pass beyond this [sympathetic] situation to the larger social organization" (Mead, 1914: 82). Thus, the transition from small to large societies—with different social strata—led to a shift from concrete relations to increasingly abstract ones. "Enlargement [of a society] seems necessary to take place by means of abstract relations" (Mead, 1914: 88). "Caste consciousness implies abstractness of social relations" (Mead, 1914: 87). In spite of this, Mead emphasized that role taking and sympathy *are possible* in larger societies, if we gain a concrete and sensitive understanding of others in all walks of life, through realistic art, literature, and mass media (Mead, 1914: 81, 83, 97-102; 1924-25/ 1964: 292; 1925-26/1964: 301ff; 1934: 257, 267; 1936: 405-417).

As social relations become increasingly abstract, they become increasingly institutionalized. "Abstractness of social technique leads to institutions. . ." (Mead, 1914: 79). Although abstract institutions facilitate relations with distant individuals, they impede concrete understanding of them as unique individuals. "Abstractness of social attitude . . . robs the individual of some social import"(Mead, 1914: 89). As social relations become more abstract, it is harder to role take with others and feel sympathy for them, thus harder to control hostility toward them. "Abstraction always carries with it a degree of hostility" (Mead, 1914: 88).

The next more complex step in development of social organization emerged in the Roman empire. Although at first the Roman empire was based on domination and subjugation (as had been prior empires), Mead stated that later "came the administrative attitude which was more of the type to which I have already referred as that of functional superiority" (Mead, 1934: 285). The Romans were not only excellent engineers and builders, they skillfully designed their social institutions to carry out specific functions. They excelled at the capacity for administration. "This capacity made the Roman Empire entirely different from the earlier empires, which carried nothing but brute strength behind them" (Mead, 1934: 285). The intelligent design of a functional administration oriented to a "larger co-operative activity" (Mead, 1934: 286) allowed them to construct and control a vast empire. This led to "the development of a higher community, where dominance takes the form of administration" (Mead, 1934: 286). Mead conjectured that the Roman type of functional administration might be of use in building an international social structure. "Conceivably, there may appear a larger international community than the empire, organized in terms of function rather than of force" (Mead, 1934: 286).

Medieval Society. After the fall of the Roman empire, the social organization and social control in Europe "rotted out. New methods of control had to be built up gradually" (Mead, 1936: 176). The church became the central institution of medieval society, and it had an ideal of what society *should* be, but it was not able to make that idea a functional reality. "During the so-called Dark Ages, Europe was in a state of constant warfare between very little groups. It was a period in the Western world in which there was such chaos, such continuous, unmitigated hostility between little groups as there has not been since" (Mead, 1936: 176). "Europe was a community in which there were ideals of social organization which were not actually realized" (Mead, 1936: 177).

Medieval society was a feudal society, stratified into clear castes that were supposedly organized according to the ideals of the Holy Roman Empire. "There was a definite caste organization of society, with serfs, overlords, and ecclesiastical distinctions..." (Mead, 1934: 318). In the medieval period, "the church was inevitably the source of authority." "It was an authority which came from an infinite deity; it was an authority which was not to be comprehended in its operation. God did not explain what all his purposes were; he told only enough to guide men in their conduct" (Mead, 1936: 11). The state and all institutions also were based on the power and authority of God: "The sword was placed in the hands of the king by God himself. All institutions were conceived of as established by God" (Mead, 1936: 11). Because mortals could not always comprehend the divine authority expressed through the church and the state, this authority often seemed capricious and arbitrary.

The Revolutions. By the Renaissance, people were beginning to revolt against arbitrary authority. There was a "breaking away from the conceptions of the authority of the church, an authority which was arbitrary." "The attitude of revolution which marks the early modern period was one against the arbitrary authority of the medieval institutions, an authority which came to them as supposedly inspired by God..." (Mead, 1936: 12). Not only did this free scientists to begin studying nature (Mead, 1936: 8), it led to the search for other types of social organizations based on human nature and human values rather than arbitrary authority. Rousseau, for example, "undertook to find in man's own nature the basis for the institutions of society." "It was not necessary to go outside of man's own nature to get the basis for such an authority" (Mead, 1936: 13). In the period leading up to the French Revolution, people began to think of establishing "institutions whose authority will lie within the community itself. The revolution gathered about the rights of man" (Mead, 1936: 13). People began to "criticize institutions from the point of view of their immediate function in preserving order..." (Mead, 1936: 14). There was a proliferation of political and philosophical theories that attempted to create a new order.[83]

Although the French Revolution was a clear attempt to rid society of abitrary authority and "the privileges of the old feudal caste" (Mead, 1936: 16), the early attempts to build a postrevolutionary society to replace the old system were not an immediate success. As a result, "the political revolution broke down. In France one constitution after another was undertaken without the result of a stable and secure government" (Mead, 1936: 51). However, there was another type of revolution that was also restructuring Europe: the Industrial Revolution. Mead traced the emergence of capitalism, industry, the exploitation of labor, and the new national and international economic relations based on trade seen during this crucial historical period (Mead, 1936: 169-198).

The Industrial Revolution brought both good and bad effects. Turning first to the good, the development of extensive trade networks helped bring peace and organization to the chaotic situation inherited from feudal times. Feudal Europe "recognized itself as belonging to a single spiritual community, Christendom. . . ." However, "the larger community was broken up, and warfare was a very large part of the interrelation of these communities with each other. The economic community, on the other hand, was a community that looked for peaceful conditions" (Mead, 1936: 187). "It brought together people who were separated nationally, in language, in customs." "It was more universal in one respect than the church" (Mead, 1936: 188). Economic relations help foster better communication, mutual understanding, and functional exchange systems, while suppressing hostility (Mead, 1934: 292, 297).

The Industrial Revolution was also a "stimulus to invention" (Mead, 1936: 184), and it brought rapid social change (Mead, 1936: 206). In fact, the social change occurred too quickly to be coped with effectively by the old forms of government; and this led to an extensive exploitation of the laboring class—including women and children—by unrestrained capitalistic enterprise. The old power structure resisted change until social problems (arising mostly from the abuse of laborers) grew to tragic proportions. In response to these problems, Jeremy Bentham, James Mill, John Stuart Mill, Karl Marx, and others proposed various social theories designed to facilitate social reform. Mead traced the development of theories and their contributions to establishing labor unions, minimum wages, socialism, communism, and so forth (Mead, 1936: 169-242).[84]

Democracy. In North America, the ideas of the French Revolution and realities of the Industrial Revolution interacted with the conditions of a people who were opening a new land. Distant from the traditional social organizations that continued to leave their mark on Europe, the Americans were free to develop a new form of democracy.

> When the colonies threw off their allegiance to the English crown . . . they had substituted a political national structure which was a logical development of the town meeting. . . . And the astonishing thing was that it worked so well. Thinly spread over a vast continent, this nexus of town meetings not only governed themselves in rough-and-ready fashion but organized states which were organic parts of the United States. . . [Mead, 1929-30/1964: 372].

Much of the American system was based on practical concerns for solving problems and making things work. (It was from this practical tradition that pragmatism emerged as a distinctively American type of philosophical system; see Mead, 1929-30/1964: 378-391.)

Naturally, the American political system was also based on the ideals of democracy, and it realized those ideals *in part* (see also Mead, 1923/1964: 257ff, 263f; 1927a: 163f; 1929-30; 1934: 187f, 220, 314). However, Mead was fully aware of the imperfections in American democracy (Mead, 1923/1964: 258f, 263). He recognized that there was a "chasm that separates the theory and practice of our democracy" (Mead, 1923/1964: 263), and was concerned with solving the multiple problems that beset our system.

Nevertheless, the ideals of democracy were quite compatible with the functional values that Mead espoused.[85] The democratic ideal "received its expression in the French Revolution in the conception of fraternity and union. Every individual was to stand on the same level with every other" (Mead, 1934: 286). Of course, equality necessitates the elimination of caste barriers. "The development of the democratic community implies the removal of castes..." (Mead, 1934: 318; also see Mead, 1914: 90ff). "The democratic order undertakes to wipe that difference out and to make everyone a sovereign and everyone a subject" (Mead, 1934: 319). As a sovereign, each person is free to control his or her own life; as a subject, each must be governed by a concern for the well-being of the whole group. "The implication of democracy is ... that the individual can be as highly developed as lies within the possibilities of his own inheritance, and still can enter into the attitudes of the others whom he affects" (Mead, 1934: 326).

These democratic ideals reflect two of Mead's central concerns: that the individual should be free to develop his or her own self—and all its unique capacities—to the fullest, but should also be socially responsible and attempt to make social changes that improve the functioning of the society.[86] "Human social progress involves the use ... of self-consciousness, both in ... effecting ... social changes, and also in the development of their individual selves ... in such a way as adaptively to keep pace with such social reconstruction" (Mead, 1934: 309-310).

What type of institutions are most compatible with the democratic ideals?[87] Mead described some of the variations in institutions (Mead, 1934: 262). The least desirable institutions are oppressive and rigid ones that limit people's freedom and inhibit individuality. "Oppressive, stereotyped, and ultra-conservative social institutions—like the church—which by their more or less rigid and inflexible unprogressiveness crush or blot out individuality, or discourage any distinctive or original expressions of thought and behavior ... are undesirable but not necessary outcomes of the general social process..." (Mead, 1934: 262).[88] Fortunately, social institutions "are not necessarily subversive of individuality" (Mead, 1934: 262). Some institutions are "flexible and progressive, fostering individuality rather than discouraging it" (Mead, 1934: 262). Mead clearly valued flexible institutions that help people to "develop and possess fully mature selves or personalities ... [and become] ... intelligent and socially responsible individuals" (Mead, 1934: 262). Freedom is necessary to allow "plenty of scope for originality, flexibility, and variety of such conduct..." (Mead, 1934: 262), but social responsibility is also needed if individuals are to cooperate and contribute to the improvement of the community: "A highly developed and organized human society is one in which the individual members ... share a number of common social interests—interests in, or for the betterment of, the society..." (Mead, 1934: 307).

Economics and Religion. As already explained, Mead recognized the value of science, realistic art, literature, and the mass media for bringing people together, fostering concrete understanding of others, and helping people control hostility, solve problems, and build better societies (Mead, 1914: 97-102; 1917-18; 1924-25/1964: 292; 1925-26/ 1964: 301ff; 1930; 1934: 257; 1936). Mead also focused considerable attention on economics and religion as two types of social institutions that could potentially promote functional social organization and control hostility (Mead, 1914: 96f; 1923/1964: 259ff; 1934: 258-305; 1936: 1-14, 169-192, 215-242; 1938: 504f; 518f). Both economics and religion are based on instincts other than hostility, namely on the instincts of "possession, hunger, or parenthood" (Mead, 1917-18/1964: 238).[89] Possession and hunger motivate barter and exchange, which are the foundations of all economic systems. Parental instincts lead to kindliness, helpfulness, assistance, and neighborliness, which are the foundations of all universal religions.

Trade and economic processes arise when two people have surpluses of different items and each seeks to exchange his or her surpluses for the items that the other person has in surplus. A farmer with surpluses of milk (but no grain) trades part of the surplus milk with another farmer who has surpluses of grain (but no milk). Adam Smith was one of the first economists to realize that both parties benefit in this type of economic exchange (Mead, 1936: 188-190). Both people exchange surpluses (which are of no great value if they cannot be traded) and get something they did not have before. Thus, "both are better off" (Mead, 1936: 190). Both parties like this type of exchange and are motivated to continue further trade relations in the future.

Not only is each individual better off, there are societal benefits from economic exchange (Mead, 1914: 99f; 1923/1964: 259; 1934: 258, 282, 287f, 291f; 1936: 169-192): Economic relations bring people together for cooperative relations that tend to generate functional social organizations. To negotiate a successful trade, people need to communicate and cooperate; in order to strike a bargain, each needs to take the role of the other and to develop sympathy for the other's position (Mead, 1934: 258ff, 271, 282f, 287f, 291f, 297-302). "In carrying out these [exchange] activities the individual has set up a process of integration which brings the individuals closer together, creating the mechanism by which a deeper communication with participation is possible" (Mead, 1934: 297). Cooperative economic relations foster the development of functional social structures, such as networks of communication, production, and transportation that unite and integrate people in functional social structures (Mead, 1934: 291f). "There is no question but that the economic process is one which has continually brought people into closer relationship with each other and has tended to identify individuals with each other" (Mead, 1934: 295). "It is a slow process of the integration of a society which binds people more and more closely together. It ... unites them in terms of communication." "Such an attitude in society does tend to build up the structure of a universal social organism" (Mead, 1934: 292).

Also, people who have developed successful trade relations seek peaceful conditions in order to continue trade, and this inhibits hostility (Mead, 1936: 187f).

> All the advances which have taken place in the modern world have been dependent on this bringing people together in terms of their needs, wants, and supplies as these are met in an economic fashion. . . . It is possible for people to buy and sell with each other who refuse to have anything to do with each other otherwise. That is, it is possible to hold people together inside of an economic whole who would be at war otherwise [Mead, 1936: 171].

Universal religions are based on the "fundamental attitudes" of "kindliness, helpfulness and assistance" (Mead, 1934: 258). These foster a neighborliness that "provides the common human nature on which the universal religions are all built" (Mead, 1934: 272). The religious attitude fosters "co-operative activity, assistance to those in trouble and in suffering" (Mead, 1934: 258). The desire to help and develop kindly relations with others provides the foundation for the religious ideal of a universal community (Mead, 1934: 271). "One who can assist any individual whom he finds suffering may extend that universality far beyond man, and put it into the form of allowing no suffering to any sensuous being." "It may be generalized in individuals far beyond one's family" (Mead, 1934: 289). Because these types of friendly feelings of parental, familiar, and neighborly kindness actually prevailed in small-scale, primitive societies, Mead stated: "The virtues presented in the Gospel of Jesus belong to the small group." "The problem of society is the carrying over of these virtues of the primitive group to the complex group, which has been extended" in size (Mead: 1914: 88). Even though it would be ideal if neighborly virtues could generalize extensively enough to unite all human beings in peaceful harmony, so far they have not been sufficiently strong to organize the international community and control war (Mead, 1929c/ 1964: 362; 1934: 295f).[90]

Mead concluded that both religion and economics have had good and bad effects (Mead, 1934: 295-298). Although economics seems to be "materialistic" and can lead to unscrupulous practices, it has proven to be one of the best ways to advance the functional organization of society and the international community, while at least partially suppressing hostility and war (Mead, 1934: 295-298; 1936: 171,

187f). Although religion is quite "idealistic," it has often divided people of different religions and nations, sometimes fanning the fires of religious fervor and nationalism that lead to warfare (Mead, 1929c/ 1964: 360; 1934: 207, 295f; 1936: 176f, 187). "The great days of the religions have been the days of hostility, between the religions, between the Church and the sects, or between different churches" (Mead, 1929c/1964: 360).

Also, religion tends to be more conservative than economics (Mead, 1934: 296), often using arbitrary authority and dogma (Mead, 1936: 6, 11-14, 289) to promote cult values instead of functional values. Religion is often based on cult values that contribute only to "the preservation in the minds of the community ... [a] faith in a social order which did not exist" (Mead, 1923/1964: 259). This is in sharp contrast with economic relations, which are not based on cult values, but rather on the functional values: "We need no cult to keep alive the faith in the functioning of money, though there is hardly an agency that has had more profound effects in bringing all men into association with each other" (Mead, 1923/1964: 259).

According to Western religion, "the final perfect society was to be a New Jerusalem that belonged to another world. The religious goal was one of otherwordliness" (Mead, 1936: 362). However, Mead's understanding of history led him to conclude that "we have been shifting our so-called ideals from the New Jerusalem to this world" (Mead, 1938: 518). Ever since the Renaissance, there have been reflective thinkers struggling against the arbitrary authority of religion and attempting to build a new form of society that is based on human nature and functional values, rather than on otherworldly ideals and cult values (Mead, 1936: 11-24; 1938: 513-519). Mead believed that the continued development of reflective intelligence and science, along with economics, mass media, realistic art, and literature, was still the wisest path of action available for understanding this world and solving its problems.

The International Community. Mead's dedication to unified models that integrate data on all facets of the social process naturally led him to a concern for international affairs, and his historical analyses reveal a good understanding of the complex interactions between nations in several historical periods (Mead, 1936; see also 1915b; 1929c; 1929-30). The prevalence of war and hostile relations between nations throughout history was of special concern to Mead, because hostile relations interfere with the solution of international problems and the development of functional social organizations. According to Mead, reflective intelligence and reason make it abundantly clear that we must cultivate an "international mindedness" and begin to think in terms of the whole, interdependent international community. This will facilitate the development of cooperative international relations and methods for solving problems without hostility and war (Mead, 1914: 83-90; 1917-18; 1929c; 1934: 270f, 303-317; 1938: 481f).

According to Mead, the most primitive and least reflective way for groups to respond to each other is by hostility and fighting (Mead, 1914: 83, 85ff, 105). "The whole history of warfare ... shows how much more readily and with how much greater emotional thrill we realize our selves in opposition to common enemies than in collaboration with them" (Mead, 1924-25/1964: 292). It takes considerable development of reflective processes before individuals, groups, and nations can see the functional value of establishing cooperative relations that minimize hostility.

In the past, war has been one of the primary means people have used to cope with international problems. It has been especially attractive because hostility against a common enemy enhances unity, solidarity, and cohesion within a nation. Political leaders have often played upon people's hostile feelings for some enemy as a means of overcoming schisms within their own country and uniting their people around a common issue (Mead, 1914: 83-90; 1915b; 1917-18/1964: 215f, 222, 227, 229; 1929c; 1934: 306). "The readiest way of arousing an emotional appreciation of a common issue is to fight together for that issue, and until we have other means of attaining it we can hardly abandon war" (Mead, 1929c/1964: 360). In the past, the power of fighting to increase social unity and cohesion provided "a certain rough psychological justification for the dictum, that at least one war in a generation was essential for the spiritual hygiene of the nation" (Mead, 1929c/1964: 360).

However, Mead asked if there might be better ways to solve international problems and unify society around common issues than by breeding hostility toward an enemy. "Can we find outside of the fighting spirit that unifying power which presents a supreme issue to which all others are subordinated, which will harden us to undergo everything, and unite us in the enthusiasm of a common end?" (Mead, 1929c/1964: 361). Although he could not give a completely satisfactory answer to this question, he made some suggestions.

After seeing the destruction of The Great War (World War I), Mead and many others believed that war "has become unthinkable as a policy for adjudicating national differences. It has become logically impossible. This is not to say that it may not arise. Another catastrophe may be necessary before we have cast off the cult of warfare, but we cannot any longer *think* our international life in terms of warfare" (Mead, 1929c/1964: 363).[91] "The Great War ... has left us with the demand for international-mindedness" (Mead, 1929c/1964: 366).

We must begin to think of international relations in rational and cooperative terms if we wish to solve our problems and build a more functional international system.

Part of the solution to war is that each nation must resist the temptation to unify its own people by breeding hostility toward other nations. "We are compelled to reach a sense of being a nation by means of rational self-consciousness. We must *think* [of] ourselves in terms of the great community to which we belong" (Mead, 1929c/1964: 363). Unifying a nation by a rational appreciation of the common goods that the people and nation can work toward is better than unifying around hostility toward an enemy. Furthermore, Mead stated that

> there *is* a common good in which we are involved, and if society is still to exist we must discover it with our heads [Mead, 1929c/1964: 364]. ... There is only one solution for the problem and that is in finding the intelligible common objects, the objects of industry and commerce, the common values in literature, art, and science, the common human interests which political mechanisms define and protect and foster [Mead, 1929c/1964: 365].

Once again we see one of Mead's central themes: Commerce (economic relations), literature, art, and science provide common interests that have proven to be effective in joining people in the cooperative activities that, in turn, build mutual understanding and facilitate the construction of functional social organizations. As people become involved in these positive activities, they will come to appreciate the reasons for developing nonhostile international relations.

Another part of the solution to war lies in increasing national stability: "Stable nations do not feel the need [to fight] in any such degree as those that are seeking stability" (Mead, 1929c/1964: 367). Unstable nations need enemies in order to unify their people behind a common issue, hence are more willing to fight over questions of national honor, special interests, and national self-respect than are stable nations (Mead, 1929c/1964: 368). Although Mead asked whether questions of national honor and self-respect might be resolved rationally, by adjudication (Mead, 1929c/1964: 368), he concluded that reasoning about national honor was less likely to prevent war than was building stable and functional social organizations. "Civilization is not an affair of reasonableness; it is an affair of social organization" (Mead, 1929c/1964: 369). Stable social organizations that function well for all members of the society provide common causes that unite the people in a cooperative manner, without the need for creating enemies and wars. When this happens, the community becomes an integrated whole that unifies all the individual selves of the group. "The selfhood of a community depends upon such an organization that common goods do become the ends of the individuals of the community. We know that these common goods are there, and in some considerable degree we can and do make them our individual ends and purposes..." (Mead, 1929c/1964: 369). The goal is to focus on the common goods (found in economic relations, literature, art, and science), organize society for attaining them, and help people appreciate their value—because these functional values are superior to the cult values involved with hostility and war. Also, seeing how dysfunctional war is will help us "cast off the cult of warfare" (Mead, 1929c/1964: 363).

Although progress has been made in building functional societies, "there are still great gaps in our social organization..." (Mead, 1929c/1964: 369). As long as major gaps and problems exist and society is not oriented to common goods that are valued by the people, some people are likely to use social hostility as a means of attacking the problem and unifying a group of followers behind their cause. "We will get rid of the mechanism of warfare only as our common life permits the individual to identify his own ends and purposes with those of the community of which he is a part..." (Mead, 1929c/1964: 370). Yet all this awaits a higher state in the evolution of selves and societies, when people use reflective intelligence to appreciate the interrelatedness of all the parts of social systems and organize to build more functional social organizations. "The realization of the self in the intelligent performance of a social function remains the higher stage in the case of nations as of individuals" (Mead, 1934: 317).

* * *

This and the prior chapter have shown both Mead's general approach to macro societal processes and his views on a variety of specific macro issues. His macro theories are completely compatible with his views on biology and social psychology, and all elements of his theoretical system are fully integrated. Society is needed for the emergence of minds and selves from the biological substrate, and minds and selves are essential for the complex types of social organization seen in our species.

There is noticeably less detail and precision in the macro facets of Mead's theoretical system than in the micro. This can be due, in part, to the fact that Mead's early work was primarily focused on micro topics and only in the later decades of his life did he turn greater attention to macro issues. Also, as a philosopher, he was not as closely involved with the empirical research on macro topics as were social scientists who had specialized on macro issues. Although Mead did not develop the macro side of his theoretical system as fully as he did the micro, he did demonstrate how micro and macro can be interwoven in a unified whole. In addition, Mead was deeply concerned about social problems and developing more functional forms of social organization.

Part III

The Past and the Future[92]

This book has presented the theories of a pragmatist philosopher and social scientist who wrote from the late 1800s through the first three decades of the 1900s. For some readers, Mead's work may be only of historical interest. Mead himself was enough of a historian to appreciate information about the past, because it helps us understand the evolution of society and the history of ideas.

However, there is more to Mead's work than a glimpse into the past. Mead was a master synthesizer of knowledge; and much of his work has the kind of timeless beauty, elegance, and value that inspires us to read the great masters from the past. Mead's ideas are still important today.

Mead's work is of especially great value for social scientists who look forward to developing a more powerful and well-integrated science of mind, self, society, and related systems. Mead's theories have the potential to organize and unify the social sciences, give direction to future work, and coordinate the contributions of specialists in many fields. To date, social scientists have utilized only a limited portion of Mead's total contribution. There is much more that could be done with Mead's ideas. He laid the philosophical foundations for a fully integrated empirical sociology and developed specific theories about many components of a unified empirical system. This work could be of enormous value in the future development of the social sciences.

11

A Unifying Theory for the Social Sciences

Mead was a philosopher with the ability to synthesize an enormous range of knowledge. The following are but a few of the different ways we can profit from his work.

Gaining Insights. Much of Mead's work is of enduring value and is as relevant today as it was in his own time. Given the limitations on the length of this book, only a fraction of Mead's original ideas and insights could be presented here. Readers who turn to Mead's original works will be rewarded amply with valuable ideas about Mead's philosophical worldview and his analyses of a broad range of specific topics.

Updating Mead's Theory. Inasmuch as Mead's work is over a half-century old, it is not surprising that parts of it are now somewhat dated. The critical reader has doubtlessly been aware in previous chapters that Mead's work has various flaws and limitations. In the past several decades, considerable progress has been made in all the areas in which Mead worked, giving us access to an abundance of new data and theories that were not available to Mead. Some of Mead's ideas have proven to be inaccurate or have been replaced by more sophisticated views. We also realize that Mead only dealt with a limited number of issues at each level of his overall theory, leaving many relevant topics untouched. Thus, various components of Mead's theory need to be revised, updated, and expanded.

Because Mead described science as always being in the process of reconstruction (Mead, 1917; 1929a; 1932; 1936: 264-291, 326-385,

405-417)—assimilating new data, rejecting unfounded propositions, and building new models—it is reasonable to assume that he would have expected his own ideas to be modified over time. There are numerous ways in which contemporary social scientists in many different fields can use the most reliable empirical data and theories to correct, update, and reconstruct Mead's theories.

Building Unified Theories. Not only should we examine the details of Mead's theories of mind, self, and society, we should also stand back and look at the whole theoretical system and the pragmatic philosophy on which it is founded. Mead's emphasis on unified, system-type theories can be useful in helping modern social scientists build unified theoretical systems that integrate empirical data and theories on all types of social processes. More than most other social theorists, Mead succeeded in constructing a unifying philosophy and a fully integrated theoretical system that can assimilate data on all facets of society and social experience.

There are two main components of Mead's work that are of special value in constructing unified theories. As summarized in Part I of this book, the philosophical foundations of pragmatism provide a non-dualistic, empirical approach to social science that makes it possible to integrate data on mind and body, micro and macro social phenomena, along with biology and ecology. Much of Mead's success in building a unified system can be traced to his rejecting all forms of dualism and requiring that all ideas be evaluated according to one criterion—namely, the scientific method.

As summarized in Part II, Mead's writings on biology, language, thinking, the self, society, and social change provide concrete examples of (1) the methods one can use to create unified models and (2) the type of theories that can be constructed by these methods. By studying Mead's methods, we can learn how Mead organized data from all parts of the whole into a unified system and how he used pragmatic philosophy to avoid dualisms and fragmented analyses. In addition, Mead's writings on biology, language, mind, self, society, and social change—when viewed as a whole—allow us to see a general outline of the type of unified theory that could be produced by a pragmatic sociology. Modern social scientists can use Mead's method and theoretical system as models to guide the construction of more complete and powerful theories based on modern data and theories.

Mead's philosophy of science and empirical theories can be of value not only to theorists, but also to researchers in numerous specialized areas of the social sciences. All parts of Mead's whole theoretical system are interrelated, each part being influenced by all the other parts. Even a partial awareness of the interconnectedness of the major parts of the whole system can help specialists control for crucial variables in their research and synchronize their specialized contributions with the work of others in ways that facilitate the construction of unified models. Attention to the larger system would help facilitate the process by which contributions from different specialists are merged into a larger unified theory.

Unifying Sociology. Sociology and the social sciences in general are fragmented into many separate schools and specializations. At present, sociology has no central organizing theory[93] to provide unity and coordinate specialists in separate fields. The fragmentation of social science has doubtless retarded the development of a sophisticated science of society and social experience, and may continue to do so. Perhaps it is time for us to try to organize our fragmented discipline around a theory that has the potential to unify the field. Because Mead succeeded more than most social theorists have at creating a nondualistic theory that unifies data on mind and body, micro and macro society, along with other related factors, his work deserves attention as a possible foundation for building a unified social science.

Mead's philosophy and social theories have the qualities that are needed for unifying the social sciences. The nondualistic and scientific emphases of his underlying pragmatic philosophy help assure that data on all possible topics can be interrelated. Mead's overall empirical system is comprehensive—covering physiology, social psychology, language, cognition, behavior, society, social change, and ecology. It provides a flexible system for interweaving contributions from all schools of contemporary social science. Its commitment to scientific methods helps ensure that data and theories on all components of the social system can be integrated in a balanced manner, with their relative importance established in an empirically defensible manner.

Finally, Mead's analysis of various social situations demonstrates the value of cooperation in solving problems and building functional social organizations (Mead, 1917-18/1964: 216f, 229f; 1924-25/1964: 279ff; 292f; 1929c; 1934: 156, 254f, 276f, 303-311, 321f, 324; 1938: 137). Cooperation can be a natural part of the scientific endeavor: "In the world of scientific research rivalries do not preclude the warm recognition of the service which the work of one scientist renders to the whole cooperative undertaking..." (Mead, 1917-18/1964: 229-230). Advances toward more functional and cooperative forms of society or science do not imply that there can be no conflict or disagreement, but a commitment to cooperation helps keep conflict under control (Mead,

1934: 307f). The "advance takes place in bringing to consciousness the larger social whole within which hostile attitudes pass over into self-assertions that are functional instead of destructive" (Mead, 1917-18/1964: 216f). A shared concern for building a unified social science could strengthen the cooperative efforts needed for integrating the contributions from all the different branches of the social sciences. Mead and his colleagues in the Chicago school of philosophy worked in this type of cooperative system (Morris, 1970: 141f).

* * *

The potential for the further development and elaboration of Mead's form of pragmatic social science is enormous. Work in this direction could have significant benefits for sociology: Mead's general approach could be used to unify many of the subdisciplines in contemporary sociology and coordinate their efforts for producing a more powerful and sophisticated science of society. Mead's pragmatic social science has both theoretical elegance and practical utility. Not only is Mead's type of unified theory intellectually rigorous and thoroughly scientific, it is also useful in promoting adaptive social change. Mead himself was dedicated to both intellectual work and social reform; and his theory reflects his strengths in both areas. We can benefit from and elaborate upon both facets of this work.

Notes

1. This simple model is intended to show the interrelations of the key components of Mead's theoretical system. It is based closely on his work; but it is open to modification and reconstruction, as is suited to Mead's (1917a; 1929a; 1929b; 1932: 93-108) own methods.

2. It is unlikely that the whole system would ever be homeostatic. Mead (1929b; 1936: 290f, 360ff) did not anticipate such a static, utopian condition.

3. See Ames (1931), Henry Mead (1938), Morris (1970) and Miller (1973) for further information about G. H. Mead's life.

4. One year later, Mead's good friend Henry Castle took his young daughter to Germany and both drowned when their passenger ship sank (Miller, 1973: xvi).

5. Other factors may contribute to the lack of attention to Mead's broader theoretical system, such as his often complex writing style (Burke, 1939) and the absence of publications that explicitly integrate all the elements of his thought in one systematic whole.

6. Peirce (1877) was one of the first pragmatists to develop this type of analysis. Mead came to similar conclusions independently and via different methods (Morris, 1970: 35).

7. This viewpoint is visible even in Mead's (1899; 1900; 1906) early publications.

8. Mead (1936: 326-359) was careful to distinguish that the "reality" conceived by pragmatism was different from that postulated by realism.

9. Mead (1936: 411) defined progress as "the constant meeting of problems and solving them."

10. The next sentence reads: "We find greater security in the laws of stellar evolution because it knits the continuities of the atoms with the continuities of the stars" (Mead, 1929b/1964: 352).

11. Given limited space, I have provided only a brief reconstruction of Mead's ideas. Further and more elaborate reconstructions are warranted—and are well suited to Mead's (1917a; 1923; 1929a; 1929b) views of science.

12. Although Mead did not describe his methods in terms of a two-phase cycle, these terms reflect the patterns seen repeatedly in his work.

13. Advances in biology, electromagnetism, and relativity have broken down the highly deterministic views of a purely mechanical universe (Mead, 1936: 252-258).

14. Some modern evolutionary writers (Monod, 1971; Corning, 1983) use the word "teleonomic" to describe self-organizing systems in order to reduce the vitalistic implications that the word "teleology" has for some.

15. Traditional psychology had split the world into mind and body: "Prebehavioristic psychology had a foot in two worlds" (Mead, 1924-25/1964: 267). "We have, in other words, the problem of the bifurcation of nature. Behaviorism tries to get rid of this bifurcation" (Mead, 1927a: 112).

16. Behaviorism was a key component of Mead's pragmatism (Mead, 1924-25/1964: 267; 1936: 351).

17. The deleted material is discussed in Chapter 5.

18. Arthur Eddington and James Jeans had recently developed theories of the origins of binary stars and the evolution of stellar bodies, creating considerable excitement in the intellectual community. Also see Mead (1938: 485).

19. Note that Mead's interest in physiology was not limited to one phase of his work: His references to physiology appear in all phases of his career—early, middle, and late. The sections of his longer works that deal with physiology are as follows: Mead, 1903/1964: 54ff; 1927a: 128f, 141, 152f, 172-175; 1932: 65f, 70f, 75, 124-136; 1934: 19ff, 27ff, 70ff, 83ff, 96ff, 103ff, 111ff, 115ff, 227ff, 240ff, 255, 335, 341ff, 348ff; 1936: 397.

20. Mead (1924-25/1964: 282-287; 1932: 126-133; 1934: 87, 98-100) made similar points in various places.

21. Without the ability to delay action, there would be no opportunity to evaluate and choose among different alternatives: "To an animal whose central nervous system includes only a spinal column and a brain stem, whose responses, therefore, take place without delay, such a tendency to react to its own reaction to an object would be incongruous and meaningless" (Mead, 1932: 136).

22. Mead (1934: 103) criticized Watson for neglecting the complex neural mechanisms of purposive behavior and ideas. "I have been suggesting that we could at least give a picture in the central nervous system of what answers to an idea. That seems to be what is left out of Watson's statement." (Later, Mead pointed out other things that Watson neglected.)

23. As will be seen in Chapter 7, the study of social behavior and interaction is needed to explain the inner conversation of the mind, and data on the central nervous system are used "to complete the act" (Mead, 1924-25/1964: 267).

24. "The advantage of our view is that it enables us to give a detailed account and actually to explain the genesis and development of mind; whereas the view that mind is a congenital biological endowment of the individual organism does not really enable us to explain its nature and origin at all..." (Mead, 1934: 224).

25. When the central nervous system is viewed as part of the symbolic social process, it no longer needs to be thought of as merely a mechanism: It becomes an organ of thought, functioning in its place in the life process. "The cortex is not simply a mechanism. It is an organ that exists in fulfilling its function" (Mead, 1924-25/1964: 282). Through social interaction, "the cortex has become an organ of social conduct...." (Mead, 1924-25/1964: 283).

26. True to his nondualistic philosophy, Mead (1932: 52f, 65f, 76, 80) explained that all emergent phenomena exist simultaneously in two perspectives, the reductionist's perspective of the preemergent world and the perspective of the emergent phenomenon; therefore, consciousness is part of both the central nervous system and the social-symbolic environment. In this context, Mead (1932: 65f) explained that "conscious processes are physiological processes" as well as mental processes.

27. McDougall's eleven instincts are: flight, repulsion, curiosity, *pugnacity, subjection, self-display, parental instinct, reproduction, gregariousness,* acquisition, and construction. The six that Mead (1909/1964: 97) identified as being social, "without question," are italicized.

28. Naturally, arrows e, f, i, and j are also involved, as they link the individual with the social environment, but these routes of influence will not be discussed in detail until Chapter 7, on socialization.

29. "Back of these [gestural] manifestations lie the emotions..." (Mead, 1910c/1964: 124; also see Mead, 1904).

30. Mead (1934: 48-51) was critical of the dualistic assumptions underlying Wundt's theory of gestures. Wundt presupposed "the existence of mind at the start" (p. 50). In contrast, Mead (p. 50) stated that "mind arises through communication by a conversation of gestures in a social process or context of experience—not communication through mind," as Wundt had assumed. Wundt's view leaves the existence and origin of mind "an inexplicable mystery ... whereas the behavioristic analysis of communication makes no such presupposition ... " (p. 50).

31. Mead's emphasis on meaning's being "objectively there" in social interaction reflects his commitment to analyzing behavior "from the outside to the inside" (Mead, 1914: 53, 68; 1927a: 156; 1934: 8, 82).

32. Whenever a gesture is followed by a variety of acts, it can have multiple meanings. Often context cues and other gestures help us discriminate which meaning is relevant.

33. The vocal gestures of nonhuman animals are discussed in the next section.

34. Mead's example (1934: 70) was followed by a physiological interpretation.

35. "Language ... is but a form—a highly specialized form—of gesture..." (Mead, 1910c/1964: 132).

36. The apes who are learning simple "languages" use symbols in manners that have the same functional significance to both them and their trainers (Patterson and Linden, 1981; Premack and Premack, 1982; Rumbaugh, 1977).

37. Mead considered the uniqueness of each individual to be "the most precious part of the individual" (Mead, 1934: 324), even though it compromises the ideal of perfect communication that would exist if everyone understood words in absolutely identical ways (Mead, 1934: 325-328).

38. Miller (1982: 24) explains the date and origins of this essay.

39. In dualistic and individualistic theories of mind, the thinker can be certain only about the thoughts in his or her own mind, and knowing the thoughts of others is theoretically problematic.

40. Mead referred to it as "reflective consciousness" in some places (1899/1964: 5; 1900/1964: 11f; 1910c/1964: 129), "reflective intelligence" in others (1934: 90-109, 118, 141), and "rational intelligence" in others (1934: 334).

41. "There are only differences of degrees of consciousness" (Mead, 1927a: 114).

42. This assumption closely parallels Dewey's approach, as Mead himself (1900; 1903) acknowledged.

43. Mead's views on neurophysiology are clearly visible in his discussion of thought and reflective intelligence (Mead, 1934: 71, 83-87, 96-100, 103f, 106, 109-118, 127f). The central nervous system is given its proper place within the "whole act of the organism" (p. 111).

44. Although Mead (1927a: 140) recognized maturational variables as part of the determinants of infant development, he did not present a model of "normal development" or postulate developmental stages tied to biologically determined patterns of maturation. This is compatible with his view that social interactions are the most important determinants of social development (Mead, 1934: 135-164, 223-226).

45. "The human infant is born with no clear-cut instincts but only with some simple reactions—sucking, reaching, etc. Lower animals have many more and clearer responses than human infants" (Mead, 1927a: 107).

46. "We may define the social object in terms of social conduct as we defined the physical object in terms of our reactions to physical objects. The object was found to consist of the sensuous experience of the stimulation to an act plus the imagery from past experience of the final result of the act. The social object will then be the gestures ... plus the imagery of our own response to that stimulation" (Mead, 1912/1964: 137).

47. For Mead (1927a: 125, 130-135; 1934: 75-82, 105-112), these are behavioristic definitions of meaning, because meaning is defined by the behaviors involved, and the results of these behaviors: "The real meaning of the object is what you are going to do with it when you reach it" (Mead, 1927a: 132). "The meaning an object has for us is in our attitude or how we intend to react to it" (Mead, 1927a: 125).

48. Mead recognized that all advanced animals are active in seeking out experience with things in their own environment and that their activities are important determinants of their perceptions of those things. "The organism in grasping and pushing things is identifying its own effort with the contact experience of the thing. It increases that experience by its own efforts" (Mead, 1932: 121f). This is an interactional model of knowledge, based on the individual doing things to the environment and learning from its physical interactions with that environment. "The environment is there for the organism in the interrelationship of organism and environment" (Mead, 1932: 129). This interactional approach views the organism as an active determinant of its perception of the world (Mead, 1924-25/1964: 275; 1934: 214f, 245). By explaining awareness, meaning and mind as arising through interaction with the environment, Mead (1934: 129f, 330-336; 1936: 307f, 351f) avoided the solipsism of the introspective theories that see mind as a special substance that is separate from the rest of the world.

49. Mead (1900/1964: 13) observed that at this point the child could take either the "metaphysical attitude" or the scientific attitude in trying to discover the nature of the object. If taking the view of the metaphysical philosopher, the child would attempt to reach understanding through cogitation and a priori speculation. "But if he wishes to know [whether the flame is a plaything or not] he makes the bright moving object merely the starting point of a scientific investigation" (Mead, 1900/1964: 13). Children act more like scientists than metaphysical philosophers, and Mead (1900; 1923; 1929a) suggested that philosophers should do the same.

50. Modern research has shown that language acquisition is considerably more complex than Mead's analysis suggests.

51. For example, mirrors provide visual images of self as if seen from the perspective of other people (Mead, 1934: 65f).

52. Copying another person's behavior in role-play is the only common form of "imitation" that Mead acknowledged. Finding fault with the uncritical use of the concept of "imitation" in the psychological literature of his time, Mead (1909/1964: 99ff; 1914: 37f, 54, 57ff, 60f, 65-72; 1927a: 144; 1934: 51-61, 65) proposed a narrow definition of the term: Imitation occurs only when a person uses role taking based on vocal gestures for imagining oneself in the place of others. Thus, according to Mead's definition, children do not imitate until they begin using significant symbols and imagination to role-play the actions of mother, father, and others.

53. Doll play is especially effective in helping the child take parental roles; see Mead (1924-25/1964: 285; 1927a: 145).

54. The actions of the team members "are interrelated in a unitary, organic fashion. There is a definite unity, then, which is introduced into the organization of other selves when we reach such a stage as that of the game, as over against the situation of play where there is a simple succession of one rôle after another" (Mead, 1934: 159).

55. Both Cooley and Mead were influenced by Adam Smith's conception of the looking-glass theory of role taking, in which each party in an economic exchange acts as if looking into a looking-glass to see how the other sees the bargaining process (Miller, 1973: xix).

56. Other methods involve a rational analysis of social systems, using reflective intelligence and science to evaluate problems and design more functional social systems (Mead, 1899; 1908; 1915; 1917-18; 1923; 1929c; 1934: 168; 1936: 365ff, 371ff). See Chapters 9 and 10.

57. "Realism is helping us to develop imagery for social science. There is place for a thesis on the relation between social science and literature" (Mead, 1914: 101).

58. Several scholars have concluded that Mead's entire model of mind, self and society has a strong structural component (Nisbet, 1974; Stryker, 1980; Turner, 1982; Baldwin, 1984).

59. Mead (1934: 143) also recognized the "pathological" condition of multiple selves where the split was too severe to allow the parts to be unified into one, single, whole self.

60. Mead's explanation of the "I" and "me" appears to contain some inconsistencies, leading different scholars to different interpretations of these concepts. Given the constraints on the length of this book, I have attempted to present Mead's most central ideas on the "I" and "me" and deemphasize the inconsistencies.

61. "I do not mean to raise the metaphysical question of how a person can be both 'I' and 'me'..." (Mead, 1934: 173). Mead did not conceive of the "I" and "me" in dualistic terms, but rather viewed both as parts of an integrated whole. "The two are separated in the process but they belong together in the sense of being parts of a whole" (p. 178).

62. This differs from theories of human nature that assume that humans are inherently lustful, selfish, aggressive, or antisocial.

63. The essays on societal issues from the last 16 years of his life (Mead, 1915; 1917; 1917-18; 1923; 1929c; 1934: 256-319; 1938: 494-519) contained much more detailed and subtle information on macro level phenomena than did his early writings.

64. In spite of the belief in progress, the Christian view of history is conservative, since it continually predicts a fixed set of ideal conditions that were established in the past (Mead, 1923/1964: 259f; 1934: 296; 1938: 507).

65. Although biological evolution *tends* to produce adaptive and functional structures, it does not produce perfect adaptation, especially in periods of rapid environmental change (Lewontin, 1978; Stebbins and Ayala, 1985). Although most organs tend to become moderately well-adapted for carrying out specific functions, there are numerous examples of dysfunction.

66. Mead's analysis of societal problems is completely compatible with his social psychology, which emphasized that problems and the inhibition of action are the preconditions that set the occasion for reflective intelligence and scientific investigation (Mead, 1900; 1903; 1910a; 1914: 30, 45, 49f; 1917; 1932; 1936).

67. Ethical and moral values are also based on the reflective and scientific evaluation of *all* the data needed to select the least problematic and most functional solution (Mead, 1908; 1923; 1938: 460-465).

68. For example, the punitive justice system, war, and the church are largely based on cult values, as is explained in Chapter 10.

69. Although Marx's ideas were based on an analysis of economic conditions, they were partially influenced by Hegel's idealistic assumptions (Mead, 1936: 215-242). Marx claimed to know the ideal state toward which social evolution is moving. "In the theory of Karl Marx the world was pictured as inevitably moving toward such a solution of the economic problem. Marx presented a very logical—indeed, the only logical—solution" (p. 219). "The earlier socialists proceeded as if they had had a vision on the Mount which showed them what the order of society should be" (p. 240). "The movement is fundamentally an idealistic movement, for it is one that has looked toward the reorganization of society, toward a reorganization lying in the future" (p. 228). Idealistic models that promise future utopian conditions often inspire a strong following. "The international organization of labor . . . in Europe in the last half of the nineteenth century. . . . [i]t was a great idealistic movement which was essentially religious in its character" (p. 226). Although Marx offered an image of a future ideal society that

presumably would emerge through an inexorable series of economic stages, Mead (1936: 215-242; 1938: 48f, 508) doubted the validity of Marx's methods and conclusions. Not only did Marx's theory rely on idealistic assumptions and overlook the fact that the constant emergence of unpredictable events makes the future unknowable, the "iron laws" that Marx used to predict the future of society were based on early economic theories that now do not appear to be as binding as they did to Marx.

70. All scientific theories—not just sociological theories—have to be continually reconstructed as new, unexpected data appear (Mead, 1917; 1932; 1936: 281-291).

71. This scientific form of "reflective consciousness does not then carry us on to the world that is to be, but puts our own thought and endeavor into the very process of evolution..." (Mead, 1899/1964: 5).

72. We can create countless numbers of hypotheses or accounts about any facet of the world. But not all accounts are equal: Many of them—though they may seem credible—are only illusory. Pragmatic and scientific methods allow us to select the more useful views and reject the others (Mead: 1927a: 125, 162f; 1932: 37, 132).

73. People can criticize and modify their society, even in the absence of environmental problems, as already discussed above.

74. "Our recognition of this under ordinary conditions is confined to relatively small social groups, for here an individual cannot come into the group without in some degree changing the character of the organization. [B]ut the society likewise changes ... and becomes to some degree a different society" (Mead, 1934: 215-216).

75. Recent work by ecologists clearly reflects a growing interest among biologists for building behavioral, social, political and economic factors into ecological models (Odum, 1971; Hardin and Baden, 1977; Spooner and Mann, 1982). Sociologists using Mead's general approach and contemporary data on human behavior and society could contribute significantly to developing theories of this nature by interweaving more sociological elements than ecologists have heretofore considered.

76. Because much of Mead's (1917; 1923; 1932; 1936: 243-291, 326-417) discussions of science has been presented in earlier chapters, science is not dealt with in detail in this chapter.

77. Mead (1906/1964: 61) recognized that historians were increasingly using scientific methods; and he drew extensively on historical data to trace the evolution of Western civilization, punitive justice, science, philosophy, pragmatism, and so forth (Mead, 1917; 1917-18; 1929-30; 1936).

78. Mead (1938: 510f) appreciated the role of "anthropology and all the comparative social sciences" for increasing human understanding.

79. Criminal justice is one of the problematic institutions that Mead (1923/1964: 261) described as being maintained by cult values rather than functional values.

80. Scientific problem solving involves getting rid of the antecedent conditions that generate the problem, as is done in the control of disease. "It is possible at present to approach all our serious social problems from the standpoint of the control of the conditions which determine the problems" (Mead, 1938: 491).

81. Mead (1934: 238-242) assumed that the family social structure reflected basic biological needs and structures within the central nervous system.

82. In later forms of social stratification, hostile feelings toward people of other social strata—who are seen as "enemies"—has led to race problems, mob outbursts, and social warfare based on class consciousness (Mead, 1914: 86f).

83. Mead (1936: 14-242) traced the political and philosophical movements during these important centuries, showing how they interacted with the economic and social developments. This analysis demonstrates his good understanding of the relevant historical data and his ability to integrate data on various institutions, social movements, and political-philosophical ideas.

84. Mead was clearly concerned with the plight of labor in his own scholarly work (Mead, 1908/1964: 88-90; 1908b; 1908-09a; 1925-26; 1938: 454-457) and in his own life (Miller, 1973: xxxi-xxxii).

85. For Mead, ideals were quite different from the ideals envisioned by idealistic thinkers. Rather than being dualistically conceived ideals with an otherworldly flavor (Mead, 1938: 514-519), Mead's ideals were earthly goals—action goals—that "appear too precious to be ignored, so that in our action we do homage to them." "They abide in our conduct as prophecies of the day in which we can do them the justice they claim" (Mead, 1923/1964: 257). Mead's ideals were based on functional values, whereas idealistic ideals are often based on cult values, which are conservative and opposed to social reform (p. 259).

86. These two themes appear in various writings: (Mead, 1908; 1914: 72-75, 89-102; 1923/1964: 262-266; 1927a: 148-154; 1929a/1964: 341; 1929c/1964: 357; 1930/1964: 407; 1934: 167f, 199-203, 221, 254f, 307-310, 324-328; 1936: 377, 405-417; 1938: 460-465).

87. As we saw in earlier chapters, *some* type of social structures and institutions are essential for the emergence of the mind and self. "Without social institutions of some sort ... there could be no fully mature individual selves or personalities at all..." (Mead, 1934: 262).

88. In such closely organized groups, there is often "stagnation" (Mead, 1927a: 147).

89. "The social organizations which arise about these objects are in good part due to the inhibitions placed upon the hostile impulse..." (Mead, 1917-18/1964: 238).

90. "[B]ecause it was impossible that these virtues should be exercised [in large-scale societies], Christianity turned around and called human nature bad ... " (Mead, 1914: 88). Original sin and the need for salvation have been emphasized in much of traditional Christianity (Mead, 1938: 505). The failure of religion and idealism to solve the problems of this world did not cause Mead to conclude that human nature is bad. Mead (1923) believed that a more pragmatic and scientific approach based on functional values would work better than idealistic religious systems based on cult values. Also, team efforts to solve problems via pragmatic-scientific methods, the way engineers do, generate the subjective feelings of satisfaction—the "sense of exaltation" and at-oneness—often associated with religious feelings (Mead, 1934: 273-277).

91. Note that warfare is based on cult values rather than functional values.

92. Mead (1903/1964: 49-53; 1917; 1929b; 1932; 1934: 116, 119, 350f; 1936: 258f, 265-291; 1938: 92-100, 479-493) wrote extensively on the past and future, showing how we continually reconstruct both scientific and nonscientific accounts of the past and future.

93. In biology, Darwin's evolutionary theory provided the "organizing principle" that greatly facilitated the development of the biological sciences (Mayr, 1978: 47).

References

NOTE: Whenever footnotes contain page numbers for Mead publications that are marked with an asterisk below, the page numbers refer to the reprinted work as it appears in Selected Writings, edited by A. J. Reck (1964) New York: Bobbs-Merrill.

Anonymous (1982) "Functional identity of response," pp. 197-211 in D. L. Miller (ed.) The Individual and the Social Self. Chicago: University of Chicago Press. (original quote ca. 1925)

Baldwin, J. D. (1984, August) "The global theory of G. H. Mead and modern behaviorism." Presented at the meeting of the American Sociological Association, San Antonio, TX.

Baldwin, J. D. and J. I. Baldwin (1981) Beyond Sociobiology. New York: Elsevier.

Blumer, H. (1969) Symbolic Interactionism: Perspective and Method. Englewood Cliffs, NJ: Prentice-Hall.

Blumer, H. (1981) "George Herbert Mead," pp. 136-169 in B. Rhea (ed.) The Future of the Sociological Classics. London: Allen & Unwin.

Burke, K. (1938-1939) "George Herbert Mead." [Review of The Works of George H. Mead.] New Republic 97: 292-293.

Corning, P. A. (1983) The Synergism Hypothesis: A Theory of Progressive Evolution. New York: McGraw-Hill.

Darwin, C. (1872) The Expression of Emotions in Man and Animals. London: Murray.

Dewey, J. (1891) Outlines of a Critical Theory of Ethics. Ann Arbor, MI: Michigan Register Publishing.

Dewey, J. (1896) "The reflex arc concept in psychology." Psychological Review (July): 357-370.

Dewey, J. (1916) Essays in Experimental Logic. Chicago: University of Chicago Press.

Dewey, J. (1920) Reconstruction in Philosophy. New York: Henry Holt.

Dewey, J. (1922) Human Nature and Conduct. New York: Henry Holt.

Dewey, J. (1929) Quest for Certainty. New York: Minton, Balch.

Dewey, J. (1932) "Prefatory remarks," pp. xxxvi-xl in A. E. Murphy (ed.) The Philosophy of the Present. Chicago: Open Court.

Dewey, J. (1938) Logic: The Theory of Inquiry. New York: Henry Holt.

Hardin, G. and J. Baden (1977) Managing the Commons. San Francisco: Freeman.

Hebb, D. O. (1972) Textbook of Psychology (3rd ed.). Philadelphia: W.B. Saunders.

Heiss, J. (1981) The Social Psychology of Interaction. Englewood Cliffs, NJ: Prentice-Hall.

Lewontin, R. (1978) "Adaptation." Scientific American 239, 3: 213-230.

Manis, J. G. and B. Meltzer (1978) Symbolic Interaction: A Reader in Social Psychology (3rd ed.). Boston: Allyn & Bacon.

Martindale, D. (1981) The Nature and Types of Sociological Theory (2nd ed.). Boston: Houghton Mifflin.

Mead, G. H. (1895) "A theory of emotions from the physiological standpoint." Psychological Review 2: 162-164.

*Mead, G. H. (1899) "The working hypothesis in social reform." The American Journal of Sociology 5: 367-371.

*Mead, G. H. (1900) "Suggestions toward a theory of the philosophical disciplines." Philosophical Review 9: 1-17.

*Mead, G. H. (1903) "The definition of the psychical." Decennial Publications of the University of Chicago (first series), Vol. 3, pp. 77-112. Chicago: University of Chicago Press.

Mead, G. H. (1904) "The relations of psychology and philology." Psychological Bulletin 1: 375-391.

*Mead, G. H. (1906) "The teaching of science in college." Science 24: 390-397.

*Mead, G. H. (1907) "Concerning animal perception." Psychological Review 14: 383-390.

Mead, G. H. (1907-1908) "Industrial education and trade schools." Elementary School Teacher 8: 402-406.

*Mead, G. H. (1908a) "The philosophical basis of ethics." International Journal of Ethics 18: 311-323.

*Mead, G. H. (1908b) "Educational aspects of trade schools." Union Labor Advocate 8, 7: 19-20.

Mead, G. H. (1908-1909) "Industrial education, the working-man, and the school." Elementary School Teacher 9: 369-383.

*Mead, G. H. (1909) "Social psychology as counterpart to physiological psychology." Psychological Bulletin 6: 401-408.

*Mead, G. H. (1910a) "What social objects must psychology presuppose?" Journal of Philosophy, Psychology, and Scientific Methods 7: 174-180.

*Mead, G. H. (1910b) "The psychology of social consciousness implied in instruction." Science 31: 688-693.

*Mead, G. H. (1910c) "Social consciousness and the consciousness of meaning." Psychological Bulletin 7: 397-405.

*Mead, G. H. (1912) "The mechanism of social consciousness." Journal of Philosophy, Psychology, and Scientific Methods 9: 401-406.

*Mead, G. H. (1913) "The social self." Journal of Philosophy, Psychology, and Scientific Methods 10: 374-380.

Mead, G. H. (1914) "1914 class lectures in social psychology," pp. 27-105 in D. L. Miller (ed., 1982 compendium) The Individual and the Social Self. Chicago: University of Chicago Press.

Mead, G. H. (1914-1915) "The psychological bases of internationalism." Survey 33: 604-607.

*Mead, G. H. (1915) "Natural rights and the theory of the political institution." Journal of Philosophy, Psychology, and Scientific Methods 12: 141-155.

*Mead, G. H. (1917a) "Scientific method and individual thinker," pp. 176-227 in Creative Intelligence: Essays in the Pragmatic Attitude. New York: Henry Holt.

Mead, G. H. (1917b) "Consciousness, mind, the self, and scientific objects," pp. 176-217 in D. L. Miller (ed., 1982 compendium) The Individual and the Social Self. Chicago: University of Chicago Press.

*Mead, G. H. (1917-1918) "The psychology of punitive justice." American Journal of Sociology 23: 577-602.

*Mead, G. H. (1922) "A behavioristic account of the significant symbol." Journal of Philosophy, 19: 157-163.

*Mead, G. H. (1923) "Scientific method and the moral sciences." International Journal of Ethics 33: 229-247.

*Mead, G. H. (1924-1925) "The genesis of the self and social control." International Journal of Ethics 35: 251-277.

*Mead, G. H. (1925-1926) "The nature of aesthetic experience." International Journal of Ethics 36: 382-393.

Mead, G. H. (1927a) "1927 class lectures in social psychology," pp. 106-175 in D. L. Miller (ed., 1982 compendium) The Individual and the Social Self. Chicago: University of Chicago Press.

*Mead, G. H. (1927b) "The objective reality of perspectives," pp. 75-85 in E. S. Brightman (ed.) Proceedings of the Sixth International Congress of Philosophy. New York: Longman, Green.

*Mead, G. H. (1929a) "A pragmatic theory of truth," pp. 65-88 in Studies in the Nature of Truth. Publications in Philosophy (vol. 11), University of California.

*Mead, G. H. (1929b) "The nature of the past," pp. 235-242 in J. Coss (ed.) Essays in Honor of John Dewey. New York: Henry Holt.

*Mead, G. H. (1929c) "National-mindedness and international-mindedness." International Journal of Ethics 39: 385-407.

*Mead, G. H. (1929-1930) "The philosophies of Royce, James, and Dewey in their American setting." International Journal of Ethics 40: 211-231.

*Mead, G. H. (1930a) "Philanthropy from the point of view of ethics," pp. 133-148 in E. Faris et al. (eds.) Intelligent Philanthropy. Chicago: University of Chicago Press.

Mead, G. H. (1930b) "Cooley's contribution to American social thought." American Journal of Sociology 35: 693-706.

Mead, G. H. (1932) in A. E. Murphy (ed.) The Philosophy of the Present. Chicago: Open Court.

Mead, G. H. (1934) in C. W. Morris (ed.) Mind, Self, and Society. Chicago: University of Chicago Press.

Mead, G. H. (1936) in M. H. Moore (ed.) Movements of Thought in the Nineteenth Century. Chicago: University of Chicago Press.

Mead, G. H. (1938) in C. W. Morris (ed.) The Philosophy of the Act. Chicago: University of Chicago Press.

Mead, H.C.A.M. (1938) "Biographical notes," pp. lxxv-lxxix in C. W. Morris (ed.) The Philosophy of the Act. Chicago, University of Chicago Press.

Miller, D. L. (1973) George Herbert Mead: Self, Language, and the World. Austin: University of Texas Press.

Miller, D. L. (1982). The Individual and the Social Self. Chicago: University of Chicago Press.

Monod, J. (1971) Chance and Necessity. New York: Random House.

Moore, E. C. (1961) American Pragmatism: Peirce, James, and Dewey. New York: Columbia University Press.

Morris, C. (1970) The Pragmatic Movement in American Philosophy. New York: George Braziller.

Nisbet, R. A. (1974) The Sociology of Emile Durkheim. New York: Oxford.

Odum, H. T. (1971) Environment, Power, and Society. New York: Wiley-Interscience.

Patterson, F. and E. Linden (1981) The Education of Koko. New York: Holt, Rinehart & Winston.

Peirce, C. S. (1877) "The fixation of belief." Popular Science Monthly 12: 1-15.

Premack, A. J. and D. Premack (1983) The Mind of an Ape. New York: W.W. Norton.

Ratner, J. (1963) "Foreword," pp. 9-15 in J. Ratner (ed.) Philosophy, Psychology, and Social Practice. New York: Capricorn Books. .

Rossi, A. (1984) "Gender and parenthood." American Sociological Review 49: 1-19.

Rumbaugh, D. [Ed.] (1977) Language Learning by a Chimpanzee: The Lana Project. New York: Academic.

Sahakian, W. S. (1974) Systematic Social Psychology. New York: Chandler.

Spooner, B. and H. S. Mann (1982) Desertification and Development. New York: Academic.

Stebbins, G. L. and F. J. Ayala (1985) "The evolution of Darwinism." Scientific American 253, 1: 72-82.

Stryker, S. (1980) Symbolic Interactionism: A Social Structural Version. Menlo Park, CA: Benjamin/Cummings.

Turner, J. H. (1982) "A note on George Herbert Mead's behavioral theory of social structure." Journal for the Theory of Social Behaviour 12: 213-222.

About the Author

JOHN D. BALDWIN received his B.A. and Ph.D. from the Johns Hopkins University (1963 and 1967), and has been with the Department of Sociology at the University of California at Santa Barbara ever since. He has done research and written extensively on the social behavior of primates in natural environments, social learning theory, the learning of exploration, play and creativity, modern behaviorism, and the work of George Herbert Mead.